The Soft Unbinding

The Whispering Canopy: Reclaiming Your Voice and the Art of Sensual Talk

MARCIA BNOOSE

ABOUT THE AUTHOR

Marcia Anita Hobbs is a multifaceted author, human rights advocate, and the creative force behind the Barbwire Noose brand. With a dedicated advocacy timeline spanning from 2004 - ongoing, she has focused her career on championing legislative reform, individual sovereignty, and human rights—themes that are heavily reflected in her ongoing academic pursuit of a Bachelor of Laws/University studies.

As the author of profound works including UNBOUND: Healing Beyond Judgment and The Weight of Empty Hands, You are the Ecosystem and more, Marcia brings a gritty, witty, and deeply compassionate voice to the complex landscape of trauma recovery. Her writing empowers readers to reclaim their autonomy without shame.

Her multidisciplinary qualifications include professional diplomas in Management, Politics and Governance, Arts (Music Production), and Fashion and Sustainability, reflecting her deep understanding of holistic, interconnected systems (crisis counselling and sex therapy). Furthermore, her twenty-plus years of professional experience as a dedicated aquatics and swimming teacher have deeply informed her somatic approach to healing. This extensive background in teaching physical movement and breath control uniquely equips her to understand how the body interacts with its environment, reinforcing the powerful, fluid ecosystem metaphors central to her therapeutic writing.

The concepts and practices shared in The Soft Unbinding (Book 2): The Whispering Canopy are offered with the deepest respect for your evolving ecosystem. As established in our first journey, this book is designed for educational and self-directed somatic practices. Engaging with this material does not establish a therapist-client relationship. You are the ultimate authority on your own ecosystem; pace yourself, and prioritize your safety above all else.

You can connect with Marcia, learn more about her projects at www.talk2meonline.com and www.barbwirenoose.com.

BOOK TWO

THE SOFT UNBINDING - THE WHISPERING CANOPY: RECLAIMING YOUR VOICE AND THE ART OF SENSUAL TALK

Copyright © 'Marcia Anita Hobbs (BNoose)' 2026

This work depicts actual events in the life of the author as truthfully as recollection permits.
This is a work of nonfiction. No names have been changed, no characters invented, no events fabricated.

The right of 'Marcia Anita Hobbs (BNoose)' to be identified as the author of this work has been asserted by the author in accordance with the Copyright Act 1968 – SECT 35, Ownership of copyright in original works (AUS).

All rights reserved. No part of this publication may be reproduced, stored in a retrieval system, or transmitted in any form or by any means, electronic, mechanical, photocopying, recording, or otherwise, without the prior permission of the author and/or publishers.

Any person who commits any unauthorised act in relation to this publication may be liable to criminal prosecution and civil claims for damages.

THE SOFT UNBINDING - The Whispering Canopy: Reclaiming Your Voice and the Art of Sensual Talk

www.barbwirenoose.com
Barbwire Noose® Pty Ltd AUSTRALIA

DEDICATION

To everyone I love and to Justice for All.

For everyone who believes in the Universal Declaration of Human Rights, shall Good always prevail over evil.

ACKNOWLEDGEMENTS

To the survivor, victim, child, adult or other. I see you, I hear you - together we make 'A Better World'.

Disclaimer and Note to the Reader

The concepts, exercises, and perspectives shared in The Soft Unbinding - The Whispering Canopy: Reclaiming Your Voice and the Art of Sensual Talk are offered with the deepest respect for your personal journey. However, before you begin applying these practices, it is important to establish clear, professional boundaries regarding the scope of this book.

Please read the following guidelines carefully:

Educational Purposes Only: This book is designed to provide general information, emotional validation, and gentle, self-directed somatic practices. It is strictly for educational and self-help purposes. It is not a substitute for professional medical advice, psychiatric diagnosis, or individualised psychotherapy.

No Therapist-Client Relationship: Reading this book, utilising the exercises, or engaging with the material does not establish a therapist-client relationship between the author and the reader. The guidance provided here is generalised and cannot account for the unique, specific clinical needs of every individual.

Medical and Psychological Care: Sexual impotence, numbness, and trauma responses are complex conditions that can have overlapping psychological and physiological causes. You are strongly encouraged to consult with a qualified healthcare provider, physician, or licensed mental health professional regarding any physical symptoms, severe trauma, or persistent emotional distress. If you are currently in therapy, it is highly recommended that you discuss the concepts in this book with your therapist to ensure they align with your clinical treatment plan.

Trauma Sensitivity and Self-Pacing: This book directly addresses sexual trauma, physiological freeze responses, and the emotional aftermath of boundary violations. While the tone is gentle, interacting with these topics can cause intense emotional reactions or trigger traumatic memories. You are the ultimate authority on your own ecosystem. You are encouraged to pace yourself, skip sections that feel overwhelming, and put the book down entirely if you feel emotionally unsafe.

Personal Responsibility: The author and publisher are not responsible for any specific outcomes, emotional responses, or relational changes that may occur as a result of applying the ideas or exercises contained in this book. The practices are offered as gentle invitations, and engaging with them is done entirely at your own discretion and risk.

Emergency Support: This book is a guide for tending your inner landscape, but if you are experiencing an active mental health crisis, severe distress, or are in an unsafe environment, this book is not sufficient support. Please reach out to local emergency services, a crisis hotline, or a medical professional immediately.

Healing is deeply personal work. By choosing to read this book, you acknowledge that you are the sovereign caretaker of your own ecosystem, and you agree to prioritise your safety and well-being above all else.

Introduction: Welcome to Your Ecosystem

The Promise: Setting a tone of absolute safety. No pressure, no aggressive goals (like "curing" impotence in 10 days), and no judgment.

Defining the Wide Scope: Expanding the definition of "sex" beyond performative acts or strict physical mechanics to include energy, breath, emotional intimacy, and sensual play.

How to Use This Book: Encouraging readers to put the book down when they feel overwhelmed, treating the reading process itself as an exercise in boundaries and self-pacing.

In our first journey, we did the courageous work of sitting with the weight of our empty hands. We dismantled the panic-inducing stairwell of sexual escalation and stepped out into the wide, quiet sky of our sensuality.

If you are opening this second book, it is likely because the ice in your forest has begun to thaw. But as the sap begins to rise, a new challenge emerges: How do we speak in this new spring? For many of us, "sexy talk" is heavily entangled with the performative scripts, triggering dialogue, awkward moments, or narratives that just don't fit us. We imagine it has to be a heavily choreographed monologue or seductive. But true sensual communication is not about dialogue; it is about delivery. About how you put 'it' out there.

The gentle breeze moving through the canopy is about enhancing body confidence, boosting your partner's ego, and cultivating the "simmer" in everyday settings.
Furthermore, we are going to learn that "talk" isn't always spoken. It is the silent, highly inclusive language of a lingering gaze or a specific touch. From the short and sweet banter of everyday life to the quiet shared space of a shower, we are going to learn how to water the roots of your connection, and we are going to have a lot of fun doing it.

CHAPTERS

Chapter 1: The Micro-Flirt (Dropping the Scripted Voice)

When we think of "sexy talk," our minds often default to the cinematic performances we see in media. We believe we must suddenly transform into a hyper-confident character to validate our partner's desire. When you try to force words that do not belong to you, your jaw locks. You feel incredibly clunky and overwhelmed.

To find your true voice, we must explicitly drop the monologue. Sensual talk does not have to be a paragraph. In fact, the most effective ego-boosters are often the shortest. We call this the Micro-Flirt.

Short, Sweet, and Unapologetic

When your partner has stood patiently by you in the snow, verbalising your appreciation is a profoundly intimate—and incredibly fun—act. But it doesn't require therapy-speak. Breaking the tension with playful simplicity is the ultimate unbinding.

It's walking past them in the hallway and simply dropping a, "Nice ass." It's looking at them from across the kitchen and giving them a classic, Joey Tribbiani-style (*'Friends'* USA Television hit), "How you doin'?" It is as simple as catching their eye and saying, "You cute."

These micro-flirts are zero-stakes. They demand absolutely nothing, but they immediately inject a lighthearted, simmering warmth into the ecosystem. They unshame the body by offering your partner a playful appreciation that makes them smile and feel seen.

A Gentle Grounding Practice: The Vocal Hum Before we can speak to others, we must feel the vibration of our own voice.

Find your base: Sit comfortably and place one hand lightly over your throat.

The vibration: As you exhale, keep your lips gently closed and make a low, steady "hmmmm" sound. Feel the vibration under your hand.

The affirmation: Silently tell yourself, "My voice is safe. I am allowed to be playful and keep it simple. I do not have to perform."

Chapter 2: The Daily Simmer (Everyday Vibes & Non-Verbal Talk)

Intimacy is not confined to the mattress. In fact, for a healing ecosystem, the most profound connections often happen in the brilliantly mundane spaces of everyday life.

The "Thank You For Doing the Dishes" Scenario

Imagine a typical evening. Your partner is standing at the sink, washing the dishes. You can walk up behind them, slide a hand lightly across their lower back, and whisper, "Damn, you handling business around here is Sexy." Or, leaning into that dynamic of acknowledging their care: "Doing the dishes? That is exactly what I like to see." You are entirely clothed. There is soap on their hands. The "exit door" is wide open.

The Language of the Shower

Communication is highly inclusive, and sometimes the best "sexy talk" involves no words at all. The bathroom is a fantastic neutral zone for this.
The Silent Observer: Lean against the doorframe and simply watch your partner shower. Let your eyes do the talking. A warm, appreciative gaze communicates volumes of desire without demanding a single physical escalation.

Washing Each Other: Step into the water together with the explicit agreement that the only goal is cleanliness and care. Slowly washing your partner's back or washing their hair is a deeply grounding, incredibly intimate form of non-verbal communication that soothes the nervous system while keeping the daily simmer alive.

A Gentle Grounding Practice: The Auditory Anchor

Notice the sound: The next time you are in a room with your partner doing mundane tasks, tune into their acoustic reality.

The internal vocalisation: Before you speak out loud, practice the sensual talk in your head.

Silently form the words: "God, you are so sexy when you're focused." Let that playful thought generate a tiny, simmering warmth in your chest before you say it.

Chapter 3: The Transitional Spaces (The Car & The Drive Home)

The car is a magnificent, heavily underutilised ecosystem. It is a contained, forward-moving pod where you are sitting shoulder-to-shoulder, looking out at a shared horizon.

Building Anticipation in the Passenger Seat

Because the car restricts physical escalation, the nervous system feels a profound sense of containment and security. This makes it the safest possible place to practice sensual communication. On the drive home from running errands, you can practice dropping the armour of silence.

"The way your hands grip that steering wheel...
mmmhhhmmm." Because your partner is driving,
they do not have to make intense eye contact,
which is often a massive relief for a skittish
nervous system. You are building anticipation,
letting the erotic life force hum gently in the
background.

**A Gentle Grounding Practice: The Horizon
Whisper**
The physical setup: While in the passenger seat,
look straight out the windshield.

The low-stakes offering: In a soft, teasing voice,
offer one sensual observation. "You look incredibly
hot driving us right now."

The pause: Let the words hang in the air. Do not
demand a response. Simply enjoy the contained,
parallel warmth of the car.

**Chapter 4: The Empty Clearing (A Night
Without Kids)**
For parents, the house is a bustling, demanding
environment. When a rare night without kids
presents itself, the immediate societal pressure is
to "make the most of it" by having spectacular,
cinematic intimacy. The ticking clock of urgency
returns with a vengeance.

Reclaiming the Space
The soft unbinding requires you to look at this empty house and declare a ceasefire with your bodies. The most sensual thing you can communicate on a night alone is a total release of pressure: "We've got the whole night, and I just want to lay here and enjoy you."

The Sensual Micro-Touch
When the house is finally yours, combine your playful words with highly intentional, non-verbal touches that map the "neutral zones" we learned about in Book 1, but with a new, sensual energy.

The Chin & Ear: While sitting on the couch, lightly brush your index finger just under their chin, or slowly trace the curve around the back of their ear. These areas are incredibly sensitive but rarely carry the heavy expectations of the chest or pelvis.

The Palm Trace: Take their hand and slowly, deliberately rub your fingers in circles on the palm of their hand. The palm is packed with nerve endings, giving this simple action a profoundly sensual feel that wakes up the body without sounding any alarms.

A Gentle Grounding Practice: The Spoken Inventory

The vocal texture tour: While engaging in that sensual palm trace, take turns offering verbal affirmations.

The offering: "Those shoulders look so good in that shirt." Or, "Your lips are completely distracting right now." * The receipt: The partner simply takes a deep breath, smiles, and says, "Thank you." You are building a sanctuary where flirting is safe, fun, and tactile.

Chapter 5: The Bedroom Sanctuary (Vocalising the Bloom)

When your ecosystem feels profoundly safe, and the wildlife of your responsive desire has finally stepped tentatively into the clearing, the bedroom transforms from a sleeping space into a true sanctuary.

The Erotic Whisper

Sensual talk in the bedroom, when untethered from the pressure to climax, becomes a playground of the senses. It is the verbalisation of the "Simmering Anchor".

Instead of performing a script, focus entirely on narrating the physical pleasure and playfully teasing your partner.

Keep it short, sweet, and anchored in the moment:

"Mmm, right there. Don't stop."

"Your hands feel so good on my skin."

"You have no idea what you do to me, do you?"

This is the deepest intimacy. It is the language of a survivor who has reclaimed their landscape, remembered how to play, and learned to speak the language of touch. By speaking your truth in these soft, fun spaces, you remind your partner and your own roots that the winter is over, and it's time to simply enjoy the spring.

Summary

(Understanding Trauma and The Pause)

For the vast majority of our lives, the bedroom is simply a functional space. It is where we drop our clothes, charge our phones, and surrender to exhaustion at the end of a long day. But when a relationship is actively navigating the complex, often chaotic terrain of intimacy after trauma, the bedroom ceases to be a mere room. It becomes a highly charged, heavy pressure space.

If we are continuing our brutally honest assessment of the healing journey, we must acknowledge the invisible threshold that exists at the bedroom door. You can successfully navigate the Daily Simmer in the kitchen. You can absolutely master the unapologetic swagger of the Passing Graze in the hallway. You can even conquer the Transitional Space of the car, throwing out cheeky micro-flirts with the confidence of a rockstar. But the moment your hand touches the doorknob of the bedroom, a profound psychological shift occurs.

For a nervous system that has been entrenched in survival mode, the bedroom is the room where the "goalpost" lives. It is the room where the heavy, unyielding legislation of performative sex is traditionally enforced. The mattress is not viewed as a place of rest or play; it is viewed as a high-stakes testing ground where you are expected to

deliver a flawless, deeply passionate athletic performance.
Because of this deeply ingrained cultural script, the bedroom has likely been the site of your most profound silences. When you have felt pressured, overwhelmed, or triggered in the past, your body's natural defence mechanism was to shut down the vocal cords. You learned to hold your breath, endure the moment, and stare at the ceiling in complete, suffocating quiet.

Reclaiming your sexual landscape requires a radical, defiant overhaul of this specific geography. You have to take the heavy gavel out of the bedroom, smash the scoreboard to pieces, and declare the space an absolute Sanctuary.
A sanctuary is a place of refuge. It is a place where you are entirely safe from the demands of the outside world. And when you finally step back into this sanctuary with your partner, fully unbound and ready to engage the erotic life force, your most powerful tool for maintaining that safety is your true-grit, unapologetic, and playful voice.

This chapter is about Vocalising the Bloom. It is about taking the short, sweet, zero-stakes energy we cultivated in the hallway and bringing it directly between the sheets. It is about dropping the exhausting burden of "dirty talk" and replacing it with real-time, highly effective sensual navigation.

The Myth of the Pornographic Monologue
When we finally feel ready to introduce vocalisation into our physical intimacy, we often immediately sabotage ourselves by referencing

the absolute worst possible source material: cinematic and adult media.

We are culturally conditioned to believe that "sexy talk" in the bedroom requires a highly specific, heavily choreographed script. We think we have to sound like professional actors. We assume we need to deliver breathy, poetic monologues about the depths of our lust, or aggressively explicit demands that feel entirely foreign to our actual personalities.

When you try to wear a vocal costume that doesn't fit you, your nervous system immediately recognises the fraud. The moment you try to force a line that sounds like it belongs in a cheap romance novel, your jaw will lock, your throat will close, and the deeply familiar, panic-inducing wave of awkwardness will wash over you. You will feel ridiculous, and that feeling of ridiculousness will instantly kill the simmer.

Let's be very clear: true, unbridled sensuality does not require a monologue. It does not require a script. In fact, when you are healing, long sentences are the enemy of presence. When you are trying to construct a grammatically correct, highly descriptive sentence about what you are feeling, you are entirely in your head. You have abandoned your body to go play author in your brain.

To vocalise the Bloom, we must return to the absolute brilliance of the lighthearted approach:

keep it short, keep it punchy, and keep it incredibly grounded.

Narrating the Now: The Power of Real-Time Feedback

If you want to completely revolutionise your physical intimacy and massively boost your partner's ego without ever having to memorise a script, you must become a master of *Narrating the Now.*

Narrating the Now is the practice of offering instantaneous, one-to-three-word reviews of the physical emotion you are currently experiencing. It is giving your partner a live, verbal roadmap of what is working.

Think about the psychological reality of your partner in this environment. If they have been weathering the winter alongside you, they are likely walking on eggshells. They are hyper-aware of your past trauma responses. They are terrified of making a wrong move, triggering a freeze response, or pushing a boundary. When the bedroom is completely silent, that silence is agonising for them. They have absolutely no idea if what they are doing feels good or if you are simply holding your breath and enduring it. When you break that silence with a short, affirmative statement, it is like throwing a lifeline to a drowning sailor. It offers them immediate, undeniable proof that they are on the right track, which allows them to finally relax and enjoy the moment themselves.

You do not need to be poetic. You just need to be honest, and you need to drop it with a little bit of swagger.

When their hand moves to a spot that feels genuinely good, you do not need to explain the somatic release occurring in your body. You just lean your head back and say:
"Right there."
When the rhythm of their touch perfectly matches the slow, steady simmer of your nervous system, you lock eyes with them for a second and say:
"Don't stop doing that."
When you feel that deep, primal spark of electricity flare up in your chest because of the way they are looking at you, you offer the simplest, most devastatingly sexy phrase in the English language:
"Mmm. Yes."
These tiny, microscopic vocalisations are the ultimate game-changers. They require virtually zero mental energy to produce, but they yield a massive return on investment. They validate your partner's efforts, they keep your own brain tethered directly to the physical sensation of the present moment, and they flood the room with a highly charged, undeniable energy. You are not performing; you are simply reporting live from a deeply pleasurable sanctuary.

The Playful Command: Reclaiming the Active Voice
Trauma is inherently an experience of powerlessness. It is an event, or a series of events, where your sovereignty was violently or

systematically stripped away from you. Because of this, many survivors unconsciously adopt a deeply passive role in their intimate lives. We become the passenger. We lay back, hold our breath, and wait to see what our partner will do, constantly bracing for impact.

Reclaiming your sexual landscape means taking your hands firmly off your chest and putting them directly on the steering wheel. It means transitioning from a passive receiver to an active, sovereign architect of your own pleasure. And the most effective way to do this is through the Playful Command.

A Playful Command is a short, confident, zero-stakes instruction. It is the rock-and-roll swagger of knowing exactly what you want and unapologetically asking for it, without any heavy, serious demands.
Again, this is a massive relief for your partner. When you give them a direct instruction, you completely remove the terrifying burden of guesswork. You are not giving them an ultimatum; you are handing them an engraved invitation to succeed.

The Playful Command is delivered with a smirk, a completely relaxed posture, and total confidence. If you are lying on the bed and you want to feel the weight of them against you, do not silently wait and hope they figure it out. Tap the mattress beside you, look them in the eye, and say: "Come here."

If they are touching your arm and you want them to move to your neck, do not sit in passive frustration. Gently take their hand, move it to the exact spot you want, and whisper:
"Touch me here."
If the room feels a little too serious and you want to inject some unapologetic heat into the atmosphere, look at the t-shirt they are wearing, give them a slow, appreciative once-over, and drop a confident:
"Take that shirt off for me."

These commands are not about BDSM, dominance, or heavy power dynamics – unless you want them to be.
In the context of the Daily Simmer and the Bedroom Sanctuary, the Playful Command is simply about un-shaming your own desire. It is the vocalisation of your absolute right to take up space, to have preferences, and to direct the flow of traffic in your own ecosystem. It is fun, and it is incredibly empowering.

Unshaming the Soundtrack: Breath, Laughter, and the Hum
We must also radically expand our definition of what constitutes a "voice" in the bedroom. Words are only a fraction of our communicative arsenal. The rest of the soundtrack is composed of the raw, unfiltered acoustic emotions of the human body: the breath, the sigh, the moan, and the laugh.

During the protective winter, the body's natural response to anxiety is to restrict oxygen. We engage the abdominal brace, we lock our diaphragms, and we breathe shallowly into the very top of our chests. We become entirely silent. This silence is a brilliant survival tactic when hiding from a predator in the wild, but it is absolute poison to physical intimacy.

To vocalise the Bloom, you must consciously, deliberately unbind your breath, and you must give yourself radical permission to make noise.
You do not have to perform the exaggerated, theatrical sounds of adult media. You simply have to stop suppressing the genuine physical reactions of your own body.

When your partner touches you in a way that feels grounding and safe, do not swallow the sigh of relief. Let it out. Let it be a long, audible, open-mouthed exhale.

When you experience a flash of genuine pleasure, lean into the Vocal Hum we practised earlier. Let that low, resonant "hmmmm" vibrate in the back of your throat. That sound is not a word, but it is one of the most powerful, ego-boosting micro-flirts in existence. It bypasses the intellectual brain entirely and speaks directly to your partner's primal nervous system, signalling absolute success and safety.

The Comedy of Errors: The Power of the Mid-Act Laugh
There is a bizarre, deeply unhelpful expectation that physical intimacy must be a flawless, perfectly choreographed ballet. But when you are dealing

with two highly complex human bodies, tangled limbs, shifting weights, and the sheer mechanics of gravity, things are going to go wrong. Foreheads will inevitably bump. Knees will collide. Someone will accidentally lean on the TV remote and blast a random infomercial at maximum volume. The dog will suddenly decide that right now is the perfect time to burst into the room and aggressively lick someone's foot.

For a traumatized ecosystem, these sudden, unexpected disruptions can be catastrophic. The sudden jarring movement or the break in concentration can instantly activate the threat-detection centre. The brain registers the disruption, assumes the environment is no longer safe, and slams the emergency brakes. The moment is ruined, and the heavy, silent shame descends.

This is where your voice becomes your ultimate shield and your greatest unbinder.

When the clumsy reality of human existence interrupts your sanctuary, you must brutally reject the urge to freeze. You must actively, loudly, and unapologetically introduce humour into the room. Humour is the ultimate physiological reset button. It is physically impossible to be in a state of primal fear while you are genuinely laughing. Laughter floods the brain with a massive rush of endorphins, completely neutralising the cortisol spike of the unexpected disruption.

If you attempt a smooth, sexy manoeuvre and end up awkwardly tumoring off the edge of the mattress, do not apologise profusely. Do not retreat into your shell. Roll over onto your back, look up at the ceiling, and laugh out loud. Look at your partner and drop a zero-stakes comment: "Well, that was spectacularly uncoordinated."
If teeth accidentally clack together during a kiss, pull back, smirk, and say:
"Clearly, I missed the lesson on basic physics today."

By vocalising the humour of the situation, you are actively managing the energy of the room. You are telling your partner—and your own skittish nervous system—that this is not a high-stakes performance review. It is just two people, completely safe, having a ridiculous, messy, beautiful time together. You are cementing the fact that the bedroom is a playground, not a stage.

The Daylight Swagger: The Kid-Free Morning Rebellion
There is a glorious extension to the child-free night, and that is the child-free morning. The sun comes up, the house is still miraculously quiet, and the heavy mantle of parental responsibility hasn't quite settled back onto your shoulders yet. This is prime real estate for the ultimate daylight swagger.

When the kids are home, mornings are a frantic scramble of finding shoes, making lunches, packing backpacks, and shouting over the noise. You dress quickly, hiding behind bathroom doors.

But in the empty clearing? The rules are completely suspended.

If you want to completely unshame your body and keep the pot simmering right into breakfast, you have to embrace the Morning Rebellion. It is about taking the playful, uninhibited energy of the Bedroom Sanctuary and dragging it directly into the bright morning light.

Imagine your partner is sitting at the kitchen island, staring blearily at their phone while the coffee brews. Instead of shuffling in wearing your oldest, most oversized bathrobe, you stride into the kitchen completely naked on your way to the shower.

You don't make a big, serious production out of it. You just walk in, pour yourself a cup of coffee, give them a cheeky smirk, and confidently walk out. It completely shatters the mundane tension and reminds your partner that you are not just a co-parent; you are a vibrant, bold, deeply fun creature who is entirely comfortable in your/their own skin.

Or, if you are getting dressed for the day and they are still lying in bed scrolling through the news, you can use the ultimate physical micro-flirt. You pull off your pyjamas, turn around, and casually flick your g-string right at their chest.

You drop a quick, cheeky, "Morning Bae," as it lands, and walk into the bathroom.

It is hilarious. It is shocking in the absolute best way. It proves that the erotic life force doesn't evaporate the second the sun comes up, and it completely rewrites the heavy, exhausted script of domestic mornings.

The Afterglow: The Final Micro-Flirt
The way you use your voice immediately after a period of physical connection—whether that connection resulted in intercourse, a prolonged session of the palm trace, or just an hour of deeply connected, clothed parallel play—is critical for setting the baseline temperature for the rest of the day.

The immediate aftermath of intimacy is often a vulnerable space. The body is flooded with oxytocin, the "bonding hormone," which makes us feel deeply connected but also highly susceptible to sudden shifts in tone.

The old script might demand a deep, emotional, hour-long conversation about your feelings. But remember, we are operating in the realm of the Daily Simmer. We want to keep it light, confident, and profoundly secure. We do not need to overprocess the moment.

As you settle back into the pillows, or as you sit up to take a sip of water, offer one final, definitive micro-flirt. This is the closing parenthesis on the interaction. It is the stamp of approval that allows the nervous system to fully power down and transition into rest.
Keep it simple. Keep it Joey.
"That was exactly what I needed."
Or simply, placing a hand on their chest, looking at them with a relaxed smile, and whispering:

"You are incredible."
Deliver the line, close your eyes, and go to sleep. You do not need to wait for a profound response. You have spoken your truth, you have validated their existence, and you have successfully maintained the beautiful, sustainable heat of the simmer.

The Sovereign Voice
When you finally realise that your voice is not a fragile, dangerous thing that must be hidden away, the entire architecture of your relationship changes. You are no longer a passive participant in your own life. You are a sovereign, fully unbound creator.

You learn that you can be incredibly sexy without ever memorising a script. You learn that a single, unapologetic "You cute" thrown across the kitchen island holds infinitely more power than a forced, uncomfortable monologue in the dark. You discover that your actual, gritty, authentic voice—with all its clunkiness, its laughter, and its beautiful imperfections—is exactly what your partner has been desperate to hear.
The winter is over. The ice has thawed. The roots are secure in the soil.

It is time to step fully into the wide, unbothered sky of your own sensuality. It is time to open the door to the sanctuary, drop the heavy armour on the floor, and let the canopy of your forest finally, beautifully, and loudly whisper in the wind.

A Gentle Grounding Practice: The Sensory Echo

This final somatic practice is designed to help you explicitly connect your physical sensation to your vocal cords, bridging the gap between feeling an experience and confidently speaking it out loud in the Bedroom Sanctuary.

The setup. Lay comfortably on your bed with your partner. You can be fully clothed or not, depending entirely on the current comfort level of your ecosystem. The only requirement is that you are physically touching in a safe, non-demanding way—perhaps your legs are tangled, or you are resting your head on their chest.

The anchor. Close your eyes. Take three deep, slow belly breaths, actively releasing any residual tension in your jaw and your shoulders. Allow the mattress to fully support your weight.
The sensory scan. Keeping your eyes closed, bring your entire conscious attention to the specific point where your body is touching your partner's body. Let's say their hand is resting gently on your stomach.

Gather the emotive. Focus entirely on the raw physical emotion of that specific point of contact. What is the temperature of their hand? Is it warm? What is the weight of it? What is the texture of their skin against yours? Do not judge the feeling; simply observe it as an absolute, irrefutable fact.

The internal echo. Once you have locked onto the physical sensation, translate that feeling into a single, three-word sentence inside your head. Make it a factual report of your current reality. Silently think: "Your hand is warm." Or, "This feels very safe."

The vocalisation. Take a deep breath in. As you slowly exhale, gently push that internal thought out through your vocal cords. Do not open your eyes. Do not change your tone to sound "sexy." Just speak the truth of the sensation into the quiet room.

Whisper: "Your hand feels really good right there."
The receipt. Your partner does not need to respond with a compliment or escalate the touch. Their only job is to receive the emotive. They can simply take a deep breath in tandem with you, or offer a very quiet, "I'm glad."

The repetition. Shift your focus to a different sensory input. Listen to the sound of their breathing. Feel the vibration of their chest. Create the internal sentence. "Your heartbeat is steady." Speak it out loud.

By practising the Sensory Echo, you are training your brain to bypass the panic-inducing filter of performance anxiety. You are proving that you do not need to invent a script; the script is already written by the physical reality of your own body. You are simply learning how to read it out loud.

Chapter 1: The Micro-Flirt (Dropping the Scripted Voice)

When the snow finally begins to melt in a deeply frozen forest, the transformation is not heralded by a sudden, deafening roar. The ice does not crack all at once, and the dormant flowers do not violently burst from the soil in a single afternoon. The shift from a deeply entrenched, protective winter into a fragile new spring is a quiet, almost imperceptible process. If you have done the gritty, courageous work of tending to your soil—if you have sat with the agonising weight of your empty hands, honoured the profound, life-saving intelligence of your body's freeze response, and slowly, deliberately dismantled the heavy iron armour of societal expectations—you know this quietness well.

You have unbuckled the demand for a perfect physical performance. You have stepped out of the narrow, panic-inducing stairwell of traditional sexual escalation and learned to wander freely under the wide sky of your own sensuality. Because you have done this foundational work, the roots of your ecosystem are finally feeling secure. The sap is beginning to rise.

You are likely starting to notice those fleeting, warmth-filled moments of responsive desire returning to your landscape. It might be a sudden, sharp appreciation for the way the morning light hits your partner's face. It might be a low-level hum of physical comfort when they sit next to you on the couch, or a split-second, undeniable urge to reach out and touch their arm as they walk past you in the kitchen. The skittish wildlife of your erotic life force is tentatively stepping back into the clearing.

But as the physical body begins to thaw and the desire slowly returns, a new, entirely different kind of paralysis often sets in: the paralysis of the voice.

How do we learn to speak in this new spring? For many survivors of trauma, the throat is one of the absolute last places the ice melts. You might feel a genuine spark of desire or profound affection radiating in your chest, but the exact moment you try to translate that feeling into spoken words, the "Third Entity"—the lingering ghost of the trauma response—slams the gate shut. Your jaw locks. Your throat tightens. Your tongue suddenly feels thick, dry, and uncooperative. The words you want to say are trapped behind a wall of sudden, suffocating awkwardness and profound vulnerability.

This vocal paralysis happens because we have fundamentally misunderstood what it means to communicate our desire. We have been aggressively conditioned by a culture heavily influenced by cinematic romance, performative adult media, and cheap magazine advice to believe that "sexy talk" must be a flawless, highly choreographed monologue. We imagine that to effectively communicate our attraction, we must suddenly transform into a hyper-confident, aggressively passionate character, delivering perfectly timed, poetic declarations of lust that sound like a Hollywood screenwriter wrote them.

We view sensual talk as a script we have to memorise and recite on command. And for an ecosystem recovering from a trauma-induced freeze, a script is just another form of heavy, restrictive armour. When you try to force words that do not belong to your authentic, healing self, your nervous system immediately recognises the lie. It recognises that you are performing again. And because performance is deeply, inextricably associated with the trauma of having to fake your comfort to survive, your body hits the emergency brakes. You feel clunky, foolish, and entirely disconnected from the very moment you were trying to enhance.

To find your true voice, we must explicitly remove the goalpost of the monologue. We must drop the script entirely and set the heavy theatrical costumes on fire. True sensual communication is not about putting the armour back on to impress your partner. It is not about becoming someone you are not. It is the gentle, unhurried breeze moving through the canopy of your shared forest. It is about enhancing body confidence, boosting your partner's ego, and cultivating the daily simmer using your own witty and unapologetic voice.

And the most liberating, profoundly relieving truth of all is this: the best sensual communication is almost always the shortest.

The Rebellion of the Micro-Flirt
If we are going to repeal the heavy, archaic legislation that governs how we are "supposed" to talk to our partners in intimate settings, we are going to replace it with a radically simple, highly effective concept: The Micro-Flirt.

A micro-flirt is exactly what it sounds like. It is a short, sweet, zero-stakes verbal offering. It is the absolute antithesis of the lengthy, demanding dirty-talk monologue. It does not require you to adopt a fake persona, it does not require you to lower your voice an octave to sound sultry, and it definitely does not require you to use clinical therapy-speak in moments of passion.
When you are trying to playfully let your partner know that you see them, that you appreciate them, and that the physical spark is very much alive, whispering about how they "regulate your autonomic nervous system" or "soothe your trauma responses" is a surefire way to extinguish the fire. While those concepts are absolutely vital for our internal understanding of the ecosystem and for the foundational communication of our boundaries, they belong in the textbook, the journal, or the Sunday morning check-in. They do not belong in the playful banter of the kitchen or the hallway.

The micro-flirt is about keeping it fun, light, and undeniably human. It is looking at your partner as they walk past you in the hallway carrying a basket of laundry, slapping them gently on the hip, and simply dropping a confident, "Nice ass." It is catching their eye from across the kitchen island while they are making a cup of coffee, raising a single eyebrow, and delivering a classic, utterly unabashed Joey Tribbiani-style, "How you doin'?" It is sitting on the couch watching a movie, looking over at them in the dim light of the television screen, and stating the simple, objective truth without any need for poetic embellishment: "You cute."

These micro-flirts are a gritty, rock-and-roll rebellion against the suffocating pressure of performance. They are quick, punchy guitar riffs rather than an exhaustive, demanding symphony. They require very little breath, very little planning, and absolutely zero acting skills. And from a neurological and somatic standpoint, they are incredibly brilliant tools for a healing ecosystem.

The Neurology of the Ping: Why Zero-Stakes Interaction Works
To truly understand why the micro-flirt is so wildly effective for a trauma-impacted relationship, we must look at how the traumatised brain processes verbal communication. When you launch into a long, serious dialogue about intimacy, or when you attempt a highly choreographed sensual monologue, the nervous system immediately begins scanning the environment for the "contract." It assumes that because you are using so many words, because the tone is so heavy and intentional, you are building up to a demand. The

amygdala—the brain's threat-detection centre—
braces for the inevitable expectation of a physical
escalation. It assumes that this speech is a
precursor to an event that might cause pain,
overwhelm, or a boundary violation.

A micro-flirt bypasses this alarm system entirely
because of its extreme brevity and its inherently
playful tone. When you say, "Nice ass," and then
immediately walk away to go wash a dish or check
your phone, you are executing a brilliant
neurological manoeuvre. You are giving your
partner's ego a massive, beautiful boost while
simultaneously proving to your own nervous
system that your words are not a binding contract
for intercourse. You are sending a safe "ping"
across the radar.

You are teaching your body: I can acknowledge
my desire. I can vocalise my physical attraction to
this person. And doing so does not mean I am
suddenly trapped in a staircase of escalation. I
can speak, and I can walk away.
You are dropping the weight of the interaction to
absolute zero.
Furthermore, the micro-flirt serves as an
incredible, life-giving pressure-release valve for
your partner. Remember, your partner has been
weathering the brutal winter alongside you. They
have been doing the complex, often lonely, and
deeply challenging work of holding space for your
empty hands. Their ego has likely taken a few
quiet, unmentioned hits over the months or
years—not because you intended to hurt them,
but simply because the sudden withdrawal of

physical intimacy naturally breeds insecurity and doubt in the shared ecosystem. They may have quietly wondered if they were still attractive to you, or if the physical aspect of your connection was gone forever.

When you offer a short, sweet, unapologetic compliment out of nowhere, you are shining a brilliant ray of sunlight directly onto their roots. You are reminding them that they are seen, that they are desired, and that they hold immense value in your eyes, even if the physical gates are currently closed or only opening slowly. You are feeding the shared ecosystem with a vital nutrient: lighthearted, spontaneous validation.

Unshaming the Utterance: The Courage to Be Clunky

Even with the brilliant simplicity of the micro-flirt, the first few times you try to vocalise your attraction after a long, silent winter, your voice might shake. You might stumble over the words. You might aim for a smooth, cheeky delivery and instead sound like a nervous teenager. You might say, "You cute," and immediately feel a hot flush of embarrassment creep up your neck, wishing desperately that you could reach out and snatch the words back out of the air.

This is the shadow of shame trying to creep back into the forest. It wants to convince you that because your delivery wasn't flawlessly smooth, because you didn't sound like a movie star, you have ruined the moment and made a fool of yourself.

Unshaming your voice requires the exact same profound, unapologetic grace that we applied to unshaming your physical body in our first journey. You must give yourself absolute, unconditional permission to be clunky. You must boldly embrace the awkwardness of being a human being who is learning how to speak a new language.

If you try to deliver a playful line and your voice cracks, or the timing is completely off because the dog starts barking at the exact same moment, do not retreat into the familiar armour of silence. Do not punish yourself. Laugh. Laugh loudly at the absurdity of it all. Look at your partner, break the tension, and say, "Well, that sounded a whole lot smoother in my head, but you get the point."

Humour is the great unbinder. When we laugh, our bodies release a flood of oxytocin and endorphins, chemicals that actively counteract cortisol and signal profound safety to the brain. When you can laugh at your own fumbling attempts to re-enter the world of sensual talk, you instantly strip the trauma of its power. Trauma is rigid, serious, heavy, and demanding. Playfulness is fluid, forgiving, light, and deeply sovereign. By allowing your words to be messy and by inviting your partner to laugh with you in the clunkiness, you are establishing a profoundly safe environment where perfection is not required for connection. You are building a sanctuary where it is safe to try, safe to fail, and safe to just be ridiculous together.

Discovering Your Ego-Boosting Comfort Zones

As you practice these short, sweet utterances and learn to laugh through the clunkiness, you will begin to discover what I call your "Ego-Boosting Comfort Zones." These are the specific types of verbal validation that feel the most natural for you to give, that require the least amount of mental translation, and that consistently generate the most warmth and genuine smiles from your partner.

Every person has a different natural voice, and your sexy talk should sound like you, not a character. Finding your comfort zone means identifying the dynamic that feels light and fun for your specific shared ecosystem.

For some, the comfort zone lies in the realm of the Visual Appreciator. This is the simple, undeniable reality of stating what is aesthetically appealing in the present moment. It requires no deep emotional excavation; it is simply calling out the physical facts with a bit of swagger.
"That shirt looks incredibly good on your chest." "I am absolutely obsessed with your hair today." "Those jeans are doing you a lot of favours right now." This type of micro-flirt is highly effective because it is direct, flattering, and completely objective.

For others, the comfort zone might lie in the role of the Capability Admirer. This leans into the deeply primal, ego-boosting dynamic of validating your partner's role, competence, and presence in your shared life. If they have just fixed something around the house, handled a stressful situation with grace, or simply taken charge of a mundane task, acknowledging their capability is profoundly sensual.

"There is nothing hotter to me than watching you handle business." "Seeing you take care of things like that? Huge turn-on." "You are so entirely capable, it's distracting." This approach honors the "housewife to working man" (or partner to partner) dynamic of provision and care, turning everyday competence into an avenue for playful desire. And for some, the comfort zone is the Purely Playful. This is the realm of pure banter, teasing, and lighthearted provocation. It is the wink, the smirk, and the cheeky comment that requires no serious response.

"Keep looking at me like that and see what happens." "You're lucky you're so cute." "Stop distracting me, I have things to do." The key to all of these zones is to keep it entirely anchored in your authentic personality. If you are someone who naturally gravitates toward a slightly edgy, sarcastic banter in your daily life, lean heavily into that. Your sensual talk does not have to be draped in velvet or dripping with romance; it can wear leather. It can be a smirk, a raised eyebrow, and a whispered curse word of deep appreciation. If your natural energy is soft, sweet, and gentle, let your micro-flirts reflect that specific warmth.

Your partner does not want a scripted actor sharing their home; they want the complex, breathing, unique reality of you. They want the voice they fell in love with, completely unmasked. When you utilize these micro-flirts daily, weaving them into the fabric of your normal routine, you are engaging in the most vital form of the "daily simmer." You are keeping the pot warm on the stove. You are ensuring that the baseline temperature of your relationship is infused with a low, steady thrum of mutual appreciation, body positivity, and lighthearted desire. You are watering the roots of the forest drop by drop, ensuring that the soil remains soft and receptive. You are laying the critical verbal groundwork so that when the deeper, more profound moments of physical intimacy finally arrive, the air between you is already thick with established trust, complete safety, and unapologetic affection.

The Foundation of the New Spring
Dropping the scripted voice is not just about changing the words you use; it is a fundamental shift in how you view yourself as a sensual being. For so long, you may have felt that because your body was in a winter freeze, you had completely lost your right to participate in the erotic landscape. You may have felt that until you were "fully healed" and capable of grand, sweeping acts of physical passion, you had nothing to offer.

The micro-flirt destroys that lie. It proves that you have immense power to generate warmth, connection, and desire right now, exactly as you are, using nothing more than a passing glance and a two-word sentence. You do not have to wait for the perfect moment. You do not have to wait until you feel 100% physically aroused. You can speak the language of the spring simply by acknowledging the beauty of the trees around you. As you step forward into this chapter of your healing, I challenge you to view your voice not as a fragile instrument that might break, but as a playful, resilient tool. Use it to build your partner up. Use it to remind yourself that you are a living, breathing creature capable of noticing pleasure and generating joy. Do not overthink the words. Do not script the moment. Just let it whisper.

A Gentle Grounding Practice: The Vocal Hum
Before we can confidently speak to others—before we can throw out a cheeky "How you doin'?" without our throat closing up and our breath hitching in panic—we must first re-establish contact with the physical mechanism of our own voice. Trauma disconnects us from our vocal cords just as surely as it disconnects us from our pelvic floor or our breath. The throat, in somatic terms, becomes a locked gate, heavily guarded by the nervous system to prevent us from saying things that might invite danger.
This practice is designed to gently, safely wake up the physical vibration of your voice. It is an exercise in proving to your nervous system that making sound is safe, contained, and entirely under your sovereign control. It removes the pressure of words and focuses entirely on the biology of vibration.

Find your base. Begin by finding a quiet, private space where you feel entirely secure. You will not be speaking words in this practice, so you do not need to worry about being overheard. Sit comfortably in a chair or on the edge of your bed, ensuring your feet are planted firmly and flatly on the floor. Feel the solid density of the ground beneath your heels. You are anchored here. You are supported by the earth.

Establish the physical touchpoints. Place one hand gently on your lower belly, resting it just below your navel. Take your other hand and place it lightly over the front of your throat, resting your fingers gently against your voice box. You are creating a physical, somatic bridge between the deep roots of your core and the gate of your voice. The soft belly breath. Close your eyes if it feels safe to do so. Before making any sound, simply take three slow, deep breaths. As you inhale through your nose, imagine the air travelling straight down past your chest, directly into the bowl of your pelvis. Let your belly push softly outward into your hand, actively releasing the abdominal brace that so many trauma survivors carry. You are breathing directly into the roots. The vibration. On your next exhalation, keep your lips gently, softly closed. Instead of just blowing the air out silently, engage your vocal cords to make a low, steady, continuous "hmmmm" sound.

Do not force the volume. Let the pitch be whatever feels most natural and effortless to your throat—usually a low, resonant note.

The somatic observation. As you hum, bring your entire conscious attention to the hand resting on your throat. Feel the physical buzzing beneath your skin. Notice how the vibration travels. You might feel it in your jaw, tingling in your lips, or even vibrating down into your collarbone and chest. This is the raw, unscripted energy of your own life force. It is the sound of your ecosystem humming with activity. It is the absolute proof that you are alive and capable of expression.

The affirmation. Continue to hum on each exhalation for two to three minutes. As you feel the steady, rhythmic vibration under your fingertips, silently repeat the following affirmation to your nervous system:
"I am allowed to be playful."
The release. When you are ready to finish, take one final, deep breath in, and let it out with a soft, open-mouthed sigh. Drop your hands to your lap. Notice the residual warmth in your throat and your chest.

By practising the Vocal Hum, you are doing the essential, dirty work of lubricating the rusted hinges of your voice. You are teaching your body that sound is not a prelude to an overwhelming demand, but a playful tool for connection. You are preparing the canopy to finally, beautifully, and unapologetically speak its truth.

Chapter 2: The Daily Simmer (Everyday Vibes & Non-Verbal Talk)

There is a massive, incredibly pervasive lie that modern culture sells us about intimacy, and it usually involves a trail of rose petals leading to a perfectly made bed with thousand-thread-count sheets. We are sold the illusion that sensuality is a nocturnal, highly produced event. It requires the right lighting, the perfect playlist, a glass of expensive wine, and a sudden, overwhelming surge of spontaneous passion.

But let's get real for a second. Life is not a movie set. Real life is tripping over the dog's toy in the hallway. It is a pile of unopened mail on the counter, the dull hum of the refrigerator, and the creeping exhaustion that settles into your bones by 8:00 PM. If you are waiting for the perfect, cinematic moment to connect with your partner, you are going to be waiting a very long time. And for an ecosystem that is actively healing from a protective winter, waiting for that high-pressure, heavily produced scenario in the bedroom is the equivalent of walking into a trap. The bedroom, for a traumatised nervous system, often carries the heavy ghost of past expectations.

If we are going to radically reclaim our bodies and our voices, we have to drag intimacy out of the shadows and into the bright, messy, chaotic light of day. We have to bust it out of the bedroom and let it live in the kitchen, the garage, the laundry room, and the front porch.

This is the absolute core of the Daily Simmer. It is the gritty, witty, and unapologetic art of keeping the connection warm without ever turning the dial up to a rolling boil. It is about utilizing the brilliantly mundane spaces of your shared life to drop zero-stakes micro-flirts and non-verbal cues that remind your partner—and your own nervous system—that the erotic life force is alive and well. It is about having a hell of a lot of fun with the person you love, right in the middle of Tuesday night's chaos.

The Domestic Turn-On: The "Thank You For Doing the Dishes" Scenario
Let's look at ground zero for the Daily Simmer: the kitchen sink.
Domestic chores are universally viewed as the ultimate romance killers. Society tells us that there is absolutely nothing sexy about a sponge, some dish soap, and a crusty frying pan. But when you are building a resilient, trauma-informed relationship, the mundane is actually your greatest playground.
Why? Because when your partner is engaged in a mundane task, the environment is inherently safe. There is no looming "goalpost" of sexual escalation. They are distracted. You are both fully clothed. The pressure valve is completely released. This creates the perfect, low-anxiety opening to drop a massive ego boost and walk away.

Imagine your partner is standing at the sink, elbow-deep in suds, scrubbing the plates from dinner. The old, frozen version of you might have just walked past them to go sit on the couch. The new, unbound you recognizes a prime opportunity for some hit-and-run swagger.

You walk up behind them. You don't need a grand entrance. You step smoothly into their physical orbit. You let your chest lightly brush against their back, or you slide a single hand across the denim of their jeans—a safe, neutral zone that offers grounding contact without tripping any biological alarms. You lean in just close enough so they can feel the warmth of your breath on their neck, and you deliver the line.
"Damn. Watching you handle business here is Hot."
Or, if you want to lean fully into that classic, playful dynamic of acknowledging their provision and effort, you smirk and whisper, "A man doing the dishes? That is exactly what I like to see."
You say the words, you give their hip a gentle, appreciative squeeze, and then you completely disengage. You walk over to the fridge, grab a bottle of water, and leave the room. You do not linger to see if it turns into a heavy make-out session. You do not wait for a profound emotional response.
You just dropped a match into dry kindling and walked away.
Think about what that tiny interaction achieves.
You just watered the roots of your partner's ego. You validated their effort and reminded them that you find them deeply attractive in their most

unvarnished, everyday state. You proved to your own brain that you can be a vibrant, flirtatious creature without the terrifying burden of having to immediately take your clothes off. You kept it light, you kept it fun, and you kept the pot simmering perfectly.

The Architecture of the Passing Graze
The Daily Simmer thrives on momentum. It is about weaving a thread of electric, lighthearted energy throughout the physical geography of your house. One of the most brilliant ways to do this is to utilise the natural choke points of your home— the hallways, the doorways, and the narrow space between the kitchen island and the stove. When you and your partner have to navigate around each other, you are presented with a choice. You can politely step aside with a murmured "excuse me," treating each other like distant roommates, or you can use the spatial constraint as an excuse for unapologetic connection. We call this the Passing Graze.

The Passing Graze requires a bit of Joey Tribbiani energy. It is about owning your space and owning your desire with total, relaxed confidence. When your partner is walking past you in the hallway carrying a laundry basket, do not shrink back against the wall. Hold your ground. As they squeeze past, let your hand casually brush against their stomach or their arm. Catch their eye for exactly two seconds, flash a knowing, cheeky smile, and simply say, "You cute." If they are standing in the doorway checking an email on their phone, don't ask them to move out of the way. Step right up to them. Slide your hands lightly to their waist, gently move them a few inches to the side, press a quick, definitive kiss to their shoulder, and say, "Excuse me, Honey," as you confidently strut by.

These micro-interactions are the lifeblood of a healing ecosystem. They are incredibly grounding because they physically affirm the boundaries of your shared reality. They silently communicate to your partner, "I am comfortable enough with you to touch you casually, and I am secure enough in my own skin to initiate that touch without second-guessing myself."

For a survivor who has spent months or even years trapped in the suffocating numbness of the protective winter, initiating a Passing Graze is a massive, triumphant victory. It is your body boldly declaring that it is no longer afraid of its own shadow. It is your nervous system proving that it can handle a sudden spark of electricity without immediately shutting down the entire power grid to protect itself. And because these moments are inherently fleeting—you are literally moving in opposite directions—there is zero pressure to escalate. You are just two people crossing paths, acknowledging the mutual vibe, and keeping the show moving.

The Language of the Water: Non-Verbal Talk in the Bathroom

As we expand our definition of sensual communication, we must embrace a profound truth: the most effective "sexy talk" often involves absolutely no words at all. Communication is a highly inclusive, deeply somatic experience. Sometimes, the best way to boost your partner's ego and cultivate the daily simmer is through the language of silent action.

When an ecosystem is recovering from trauma, the physical body often feels heavy, disjointed, and constantly on edge. The bathroom—specifically the shower—is a fantastic, ready-made sanctuary that perfectly counters this. Water is inherently grounding. The sound of it hitting the tile creates a beautiful, white-noise acoustic barrier from the outside world. The steam warms the air, and the heat of the water physically forces tight, traumatised muscles to release their defensive brace.
How do we use this environment for the Daily Simmer? We engage in the Language of the Unspoken.

The Silent Observer
There is a profound intimacy in the act of simply witnessing your partner. When they are taking a shower, the old, polite script would tell you to give them total privacy, or the Hollywood script would tell you to jump in and immediately initiate a steamy, cinematic love scene. The soft unbinding offers a third, infinitely cooler option.
Walk into the bathroom to grab your toothbrush. Do not take off your clothes. Do not make a big production out of it. Simply lean against the doorframe, cross your arms, and watch them for a moment. Let your eyes do the heavy lifting. A warm, unhurried, highly appreciative gaze

communicates absolute volumes of desire without demanding a single physical response.

When your partner wipes the water from their eyes and looks at you through the steam, you don't need to launch into a monologue. You just hold the eye contact. You let them see that you are thoroughly enjoying the view. If you feel compelled to speak, you use the shortest, sweetest micro-flirt available. Give them a smirk and say, "Take your time. I'm just enjoying the scenery." This act of silent observation is a massive ego-boost. It tells your partner that their body, in its most natural, un-styled, un-performed state, is completely captivating to you. And for your own nervous system, it is a masterclass in experiencing the "wide sky of desire." You are actively engaging your visual sensuality, allowing yourself to feel the warm hum of attraction, all while remaining entirely safe, fully clothed, and securely anchored to the doorframe.

The Art of Washing Each Other
If you feel your ecosystem has thawed enough to share the physical space of the water, stepping into the shower together is a deeply powerful practice—provided you establish the rules of the clearing first.

You must enter the water with the explicit, internal (or spoken) agreement that the only goals are cleanliness, care, and the enjoyment of the heat. You are completely annihilating the goalpost of intercourse.

Once inside, use the Language of the Unspoken
to tend to each other's neutral zones. Take the
soap and slowly, deliberately wash your partner's
back. Focus entirely on the physical emotive of the
moment. Feel the slickness of the soap, the hard,
safe structure of their shoulder blades, and the
heat of the water running over your hands.
Then, move to their head. Washing your partner's
hair is one of the most intimately grounding,
profoundly sensual acts two humans can share.
The scalp is packed with nerve endings, but it
carries absolutely zero of the heavy, panic-
inducing expectations of the pelvis or the chest.
As you massage the shampoo into their hair,
dragging your fingertips slowly across their scalp,
you are offering deep pressure therapy right to the
top of their nervous system. You are physically
washing away the stress of their day.

You do not need to say a single word. The firm,
slow pressure of your fingers is doing all the
talking. It is whispering, "I've got you. You can let
your guard down here. I am taking care of you."
This non-verbal communication is the purest form
of the daily simmer. It regulates the heartbeat,
lowers cortisol, and builds a bedrock of physical
trust that is stronger than iron.

Digital Simmering: The Art of the Mid-Day Text
The Daily Simmer does not have to stop when you
walk out the front door. In fact, physical distance is
often an incredible advantage when you are
practising zero-stakes sensual communication.
When you are at work, running errands, or simply
apart for the afternoon, your nervous system is

completely removed from the immediate physical presence of your partner. There is literally zero possibility of a physical escalation, which means your brain's threat-detection centre is entirely offline regarding intimacy. You are safe in your own separate bubble.

This is the perfect time to drop a text message. Digital simmering is the art of the delayed fuse. It is about planting a tiny, playful thought in your partner's brain and letting it quietly generate heat for the rest of the day.
Again, we are strictly avoiding the heavy, scripted monologue. We are not sending three paragraphs of poetic longing or deep emotional processing. We are sending a quick, punchy, Joey Tribbiani text. It should take you five seconds to type.
"You looked so incredibly good leaving the house this morning. Just saying."
"I am highly distracted today, thinking about that shirt you were wearing."
"Just a mid-day reminder that your ass is spectacular."
"How you doin' today babe?"

When your partner receives this text while sitting in a boring staff meeting, waiting in line at the post office, or wrestling with a spreadsheet, it completely alters the acoustic reality of their day. They look at their phone, and they smile. Their ego gets a beautiful, unexpected jolt of electricity. They feel desired, noticed, and prioritised. And you? You get the immense satisfaction of knowing you just initiated a sensual connection with absolute swagger and zero anxiety. You threw a pebble into the pond, and now you get to watch the ripples spread outward for the rest of the afternoon. When you finally reunite in the evening, the air between you is already primed. The pot is already simmering. You don't have to start from scratch, awkwardly trying to generate a spark out of thin air, because you already lit the match at 2:00 PM.

The Freedom of the Unscripted Life
The profound truth of the Daily Simmer is that true, resilient intimacy does not require perfection. It does not require a pristine environment, a flawless outfit, or a rehearsed script. It thrives in the messy, the clunky reality of your actual life. You can be incredibly sexy while wearing worn-out sweatpants, nursing a messy bun, and holding a chipped coffee mug. You can be deeply sensual while picking up dog toys off the living room floor or folding a pile of towels. When you finally realise that your inherent worth and your erotic life force are not tied to a cinematic performance, the entire world becomes a safe, expansive playground.

You stop waiting for the "perfect moment" to connect with your partner, and you start using the moments you actually have. You use the kitchen sink. You use the hallway. You use the water in the shower. You use a quick text message on your lunch break.

You reclaim your voice not by shouting, but by casually, playfully, and unapologetically dropping a compliment in the spaces between the chores. You become a master of the micro-flirt, a champion of the non-verbal touch, and the sovereign architect of an everyday environment that feels warm, alive, and entirely safe. You let go of the pressure, and you invite the fun back into the house.

A Gentle Grounding Practice: The Auditory Anchor

When we are caught up in the relentless stress of daily life, we often become completely deaf to the physical presence of our partner. We live in the exact same house, but we operate in totally separate, isolated silos, consumed by our own to-do lists, our phones, and our internal anxieties.

To effectively engage in the Daily Simmer, we must first learn how to tune back into the shared ecosystem. We have to practice the art of noticing. This practice is designed to help you drop your anchor directly into the present moment and engage your auditory sensuality without demanding any interaction, eye contact, or performance from your partner.

The shared environment. The next time you are in a room with your partner while you are both engaged in mundane, separate tasks—perhaps you are reading a book on the couch while they are paying bills at the kitchen table, or you are folding laundry while they are prepping dinner—do not turn on the television. Do not put in your headphones. Let the room be relatively quiet. Notice the sound. Close your eyes for just thirty seconds and tune entirely into their acoustic reality. Treat the sounds they are making as a piece of instrumental music. Listen to the specific, unique rhythm of their footsteps as they move across the floorboards. Listen to the subtle cadence of their breathing. Listen to the clinking of the dishes, the scratching of their pen, or the soft rustling of their clothing as they shift their weight.

Gather the emotions without judgment. Do not try to analyse what they are doing; simply let the sound waves hit your ears. This signals to your nervous system that you are sharing space with a safe, familiar organism. You are passively receiving the absolute proof of their existence in your shared space.

The internal vocalisation. Open your eyes and look at them. Before you speak a single word out loud, practice the art of sensual talk entirely inside your own head. Look at the way they are standing, the line of their jaw, or the way their hair falls across their forehead, and silently form the words in your mind.

Think to yourself: "God, you are so sexy when you are focused like that." Or, "I love the way your hands look when you are working." Or simply, "You cute."

Let it simmer. Do not say it out loud yet. Just let that playful, warm thought sit right in the centre of your chest. Notice how simply thinking the words alters your own physical state. Notice if it brings a slight, secret smile to your lips, or a tiny hum of warmth to your belly. Allow that thought to generate a tiny, contained, simmering heat inside your own body.

You have just successfully engaged your erotic life force entirely on your own terms. You have tuned into the ecosystem, appreciated the wildlife, and generated warmth without a single ounce of pressure or expectation. Keep that internal feeling. Let it anchor you. And whenever you are ready, whenever the swagger strikes you and the moment feels right, you can open your mouth and let that short, sweet whisper out into the room.

Chapter 3: The Transitional Spaces (The Car & The Drive Home)

In our modern, relentlessly fast-paced lives, we spend an exorbitant amount of time in a state of transition. We are constantly moving from point A to point B. We commute to work, we drive to the grocery store, we pick up the dry cleaning, and we navigate the sprawling concrete arteries of our cities. For most people, the car is viewed merely as a utilitarian tool—a metal box designed to transport a human body across a geographical distance as quickly as traffic laws will allow. We treat the commute as "dead time," a frustrating purgatory between the places where our actual lives are supposed to happen.
But if you are actively engaged in the work of unbinding your ecosystem and reclaiming your sensual voice, you must immediately radically re-evaluate your relationship with your vehicle.

The car is not dead space. The car is a magnificent, highly contained, and heavily underutilised mobile sanctuary. It is a forward-moving pod where you are physically strapped in, sitting shoulder-to-shoulder with your partner, looking out at a shared, constantly changing horizon. From a trauma-informed perspective, the architecture of a moving vehicle provides one of the absolute safest, most structurally brilliant environments for practicing the Daily Simmer and mastering the art of the micro-flirt.

To understand why the car is such a profound catalyst for safe, responsive desire, we have to look closely at the biological and psychological mechanics of a road trip—even if that road trip is just a ten-minute drive to the hardware store.

The Neurology of the Seatbelt: The Ultimate Hard Boundary

When an ecosystem is recovering from the protective winter of a trauma response, its primary, overarching concern is the sudden, uninvited escalation of physical boundaries. The nervous system is constantly scanning the environment, asking: If I engage playfully right now, will I be expected to follow through? If I say something flirtatious, will I be suddenly cornered into a physical act I am not ready for? This hyper-vigilant threat-detection is exactly what causes the jaw to lock and the voice to freeze in the bedroom or on the living room couch. In an open room, the possibility of escalation is theoretically limitless. Now, place that same nervous system inside the passenger seat of a moving car.

The immediate somatic reality of the vehicle changes everything. You are physically strapped into a bucket seat by a reinforced nylon belt. Your partner is strapped into the driver's seat. There is a large, unyielding centre console constructed of hard plastic and metal dividing the space between you. The doors are locked. The vehicle is traveling at sixty kilometre's an hour down a busy street. The physical environment strictly dictates that an intense physical escalation is literally, practically impossible.

The car acts as an external, structural boundary. It takes the burden of boundary-setting completely off your shoulders. You do not have to consciously police the escalation because the environment itself is policing it for you. Your brain recognises this instantly. It registers the seatbelt, the centre console, and the speed of the vehicle, and it breathes a massive, subconscious sigh of relief. The threat-detection centre powers down. Because the threat of sudden, demanding physical escalation drops to zero, the space suddenly opens up for playfulness. The car becomes a beautifully contained sandbox where you can test your sensual voice, drop cheeky micro-flirts, and build electric anticipation without any fear of the interaction spiralling out of your sovereign control. It is the safest possible laboratory for the returning spring.

The Parallel Gaze: Releasing the Pressure of the Stare

In the traditional, highly scripted romantic narrative, intense, unwavering eye contact is presented as the ultimate indicator of deep passion. We are told to gaze deeply into our partner's soul to communicate our desire.

But for a trauma survivor, prolonged, intense eye contact can be incredibly overwhelming. When you are sitting face-to-face with someone, and the silence stretches out, the eye contact can suddenly stop feeling like a romantic connection and start feeling like a demand. It can trigger the visceral sensation of being hunted, scrutinised, or interrogated. The "Third Entity" of trauma hates being stared at.

The car effortlessly annihilates this problem through the magic of the Parallel Gaze.

When you are driving together, you are not sitting face-to-face; you are sitting side-by-side. Your bodies are parallel, pointing in the exact same direction. More importantly, your partner's primary focus must legally and practically remain fixed on the windshield, the mirrors, and the road ahead. They cannot safely turn their head to stare at you for more than a fraction of a second.

This parallel orientation is a psychological masterstroke. It removes the suffocating pressure of the spotlight. You are no longer on stage, performing for an audience of one. Instead, you are two co-pilots navigating a shared landscape. Because your partner is looking at the road, you are granted a profound cloak of invisibility. You have the absolute freedom to look at them—to really observe them—without the anxiety of being caught in a heavy, expectant stare. You can study the way the passing streetlights illuminate the sharp angle of their jaw. You can watch the effortless competence of their hands navigating the steering wheel. You can admire the line of their neck as they check the blind spot.

You are engaging your visual sensuality from a place of total, unbothered safety. And because you are not being stared at in return, your throat feels looser. The words do not feel as heavy.

Passenger Seat Swagger: Vocalising the Anticipation

Once you recognise the unparalleled safety of the vehicle's boundaries and the freedom of the parallel gaze, you can begin to actively use the passenger seat to cultivate the Daily Simmer. This is where you deploy the short, punchy, unapologetic micro-flirts we established in the first chapter.

You do not need to wait for a romantic weekend getaway. You can do this on a Wednesday evening while running an errand. Maybe there is a bag of takeout food sitting on the floorboards, or maybe your dog, Lando, is in the backseat with his head hanging out the window, happily snapping at the wind. The environment does not need to be pristine; it just needs to be yours.

As your partner is driving, lean back in your seat. Let your shoulders drop. Take a deep, grounding breath, feeling the vibration of the engine humming through the floorboards and up into your boots. Turn your head lazily toward them. Watch their hands. There is something deeply, undeniably primal about watching the person you love expertly control a piece of heavy machinery. It speaks to that rock-and-roll grit, an undercurrent of capability and power.

When they smoothly navigate a turn or shift gears, drop a line directly into the quiet space of the cabin.
"The way your hands grip that steering wheel... mmmhhhmmm."

Let the "mmmhhhmmm" be a low, approving, audible hum in the back of your throat. It is short, it is sweet, and it is dripping with relaxed swagger. Because they are driving, they cannot turn to face you. They might grip the wheel a little tighter. They might flash a quick, highly appreciative smirk in the rearview mirror. Their ego just received a massive, unexpected jolt of electricity, but they have to maintain their focus on the road. The tension is created, acknowledged, and immediately contained by the act of driving.
You can use the parallel gaze to throw out other zero-stakes observations.
"You look incredibly hot when you're driving."
"Keep your eyes on the road, baby. I'm just enjoying the view."

You are building a beautifully constructed bridge of anticipation. You are letting the erotic life force hum gently in the background, harmonising perfectly with the sound of the tyres on the asphalt. If a momentary wave of panic arises—a brief echo of the winter freeze—you simply look out your own window. You watch the trees blur past. You remind yourself that you are strapped in, the doors are locked, and the boundary is ironclad.

The Language of the Cabin: Non-Verbal Car Talk
The Transitional Space is also an exceptional place for inclusive, non-verbal communication. The confined nature of the cabin means that every physical movement and every acoustic choice becomes magnified. You can completely alter the

energetic ecosystem of the car without saying a single word.

The Playlist as the Wingman

Music is a profoundly effective tool for regulating the nervous system and setting an unapologetic vibe. When you get into the car, take control of the audio. Do not default to whatever quiet, passive background noise happens to be playing on the radio. Make a deliberate choice.

Put on a track that makes you feel powerful, grounded, and slightly rebellious. Turn up the heavy metal or the gritty, bass-heavy rock. Let the vibration of the kick drum and the bass guitar physically reverberate through the car seats and into your spine. This kind of deep, rhythmic vibration is actually incredibly soothing to a traumatized nervous system; it mimics the heavy, grounding pressure of a weighted blanket, but it does it with absolute swagger.

You don't need to speak. You just sit in the passenger seat, bobbing your head to the rhythm, completely owning the space. Sharing a heavy, driving beat with your partner in the contained pod of the car communicates a shared, unspoken wavelength. It says, "We are on the same ride. We share the same grit." It is a sensual connection that bypasses the throat entirely.

The Centre Console Neutral Zone

Physical touch in the car should be approached with the same lighthearted, zero-stakes philosophy as the micro-flirt. The centre console is your shared neutral territory. It is the border between your two seats.

You do not need to engage in heavy, distracting physical contact. The Daily Simmer thrives on the absolute minimum effective dose.

As they are driving, simply rest your hand casually on their thigh, just above the knee. Do not squeeze. Do not move your hand higher. Do not make it a prelude to anything else. Just let your hand rest there, an anchor of warmth and solidarity. It is a physical manifestation of the Joey Tribbiani "How you doin'?" Or, simply lay your hand open, palm up, on the centre console. You aren't demanding they take it. You are simply offering the open architecture of a clearing. When they reach over and loosely lace their fingers through yours, resting their hand on yours while they steer with the other, you have achieved a masterclass in parallel grounding. You are physically connected, safely contained, and moving forward together.

The Drive Home: The Airlock of the Ecosystem
Perhaps the most crucial, strategically vital transitional space in your entire routine is the Drive Home.

Whether you are returning from a high-energy social event, a quiet dinner date, or a chaotic afternoon running errands, crossing the threshold of your front door often triggers a profound energetic shift. The house is where the responsibilities live. It is where the bills are sitting on the counter, the laundry is waiting in the basket, and the ghosts of past arguments or silent winters often echo in the hallways. For many survivors, walking through the front door automatically re-engages the heavy armour of domestic survival mode.

The Drive Home is your "airlock." It is the decompression chamber between the outside world and the heavy reality of the house.
If you want to maintain the Daily Simmer and carry a sense of playful, safe intimacy into your home, you must actively prime the ecosystem while you are still in the car. You must use the final ten minutes of the drive to establish the energetic rules of engagement before you turn the key in the front door.

As you turn onto your street, use your voice to explicitly and playfully map out the immediate future. You want to completely remove the anxiety of the unknown, ensuring your partner (and your own nervous system) knows exactly what the evening holds, and more importantly, what it doesn't hold.

Drop a verbal boundary that is disguised as a micro-flirt.
"When we get inside, I am taking my shoes off, and I just want to lay my head in your lap on the couch."
Or, if you are feeling a bit more brazen and want to acknowledge the physical attraction without making a demand:

"I had a great time tonight. You looked sexy at dinner. When we get home, I just want to pour a glass of water, lock the door, and exist in the same space as you."

By vocalising the plan in the car, you are actively dismantling the ticking clock of urgency that often ruins a night in. You are telling your partner and yourself that the pressure is completely off. There is no hidden agenda waiting for them in the bedroom. You have used the contained safety of the vehicle to negotiate a perfectly peaceful, deeply connected ceasefire for the rest of the evening.

When you finally pull into the driveway, turn off the engine, and the heavy metal fades into silence, the air in the cabin should feel warm, unbothered, and safe. You step out of the car not as two exhausted roommates bracing for the chores of the house, but as two deeply connected, parallel travellers who have successfully navigated the transition. You have kept the simmer alive in transit, proving that your voice and your desire are not fragile things that shatter the moment you leave the house; they are rugged, resilient companions that ride shotgun wherever you go.

A Gentle Grounding Practice: The Horizon Whisper
Because the car is such a magnificent, neurologically safe container, it is the perfect environment for a structured somatic practice. This exercise is designed to help you explicitly bridge the gap between the internal feeling of

safety and the external vocalisation of a micro-flirt, utilising the brilliance of the parallel gaze.

The physical setup. This practice must be done while you are the passenger, and your partner is driving in relatively calm, predictable traffic (e.g., cruising down a highway or a long stretch of suburban road, not navigating a chaotic, high-stress city intersection).

Empty the hands. Begin by actively releasing any physical tension. Let your hands rest entirely empty in your lap, palms facing upward in a gesture of somatic surrender. Uncross your legs. Let your shoulders drop away from your ears. Feel the specific, reassuring tightness of the seatbelt running across your chest. This is your hard boundary. You are secured.

The shared view. Keep your head facing forward. Look straight out the windshield. Do not turn your neck to look at your partner. Allow your eyes to focus softly on the horizon line where the road meets the sky, or watch the steady, rhythmic passing of the dashed white lines on the asphalt. Let the forward motion of the car hypnotise your threat-detection centre into a state of calm.

The internal check-in. Take a deep breath in, feeling the vibration of the engine beneath you. Check the temperature of your ecosystem. Acknowledge the profound safety of the fact that your partner is busy driving and cannot escalate a physical interaction. Feel the relief of that limitation.

The low-stakes offering. Now, you are going to practice the Horizon Whisper. Without turning your head, keeping your eyes completely fixed on the road ahead, you are going to offer one short, sweet, unapologetic sensual observation out loud into the cabin.

Do not overthink it. Keep your voice soft, calm, and perhaps lightly teasing.
Speak to the windshield: "You look incredibly hot driving us right now." Or, "I really love the sound of your voice when you're relaxed like this."
Or simply, "I feel really, really safe sitting next to you right now."

The pause. The moment the words leave your mouth, let them hang in the air. Do not immediately follow up with a question. Do not turn your head to check their reaction. Do not demand a response. You are not starting a deep conversation; you are simply placing a beautiful, vibrating truth into the centre console and leaving it there.

Your partner will hear it. They will absorb the massive ego boost. They might smile, they might murmur a quiet "Thank you," or they might just reach over and briefly squeeze your knee.

Whatever their reaction, your only job is to sit back and simply enjoy the contained, parallel warmth of the car. You spoke your truth. Your voice did not break. The world did not end. You successfully whispered to the horizon, and the canopy of your shared forest is infinitely stronger for it.

The Soft Unbinding
(Releasing Scripts and Shame)

You survived the winter. The ice has thawed. But how do you learn to speak in the new spring?

For trauma survivors and those recovering from a profound physical disconnect, the thought of initiating "sexy talk" often triggers a paralysing freeze. We've been sold a cultural lie that intimacy requires a flawless, highly choreographed monologue, or a high-stakes, cinematic performance—especially the moment the kids leave the house. But forcing a script that doesn't belong to you isn't healing; it's just putting the heavy iron armour right back on.

Here, we, with author Marcia Hobbs—who holds a certification in Sex Therapy—completely destroy the myth of the perfectly scripted romance.

This is your true-grit, light-hearted, and unapologetic guide to reclaiming your sensual voice. You don't need to sound like a movie star to generate heat, and you don't need to use clinical therapy-speak in the bedroom. You just need the rock-and-roll swagger of the everyday.

Inside, you will discover how to:

Drop the Monologue: Master the zero-stakes "Micro-Flirt" to massively boost your partner's ego without ever demanding an escalation.

Cultivate the Daily Simmer: Take intimacy out of the bedroom and into the brilliantly mundane spaces of the kitchen sink, the hallway, and the daily commute.

Navigate the Empty Clearing: Destroy the heavy expectations of the "kid-free night" by declaring a Masterful Ceasefire and replacing performance anxiety with the Sensual Micro-Touch.

Embrace the Clunkiness: Learn why laughing through the awkwardness is the ultimate physiological reset button for a traumatised nervous system.
It's time to stop performing, embrace your unvarnished reality, and invite the fun back into your house. Drop the script. Unshame your desire. Let the canopy whisper.

Chapter 4: The Empty Clearing (A Night Without Kids)

There is a highly specific, almost deafening quality to the silence that falls over a house the moment the front door closes behind your children as they leave for a sleepover, a weekend at their grandparents', or a school camp. For months, perhaps even years, you have been operating in a state of high alert, domestic triage. The airspace of your home has been filled with the relentless, bustling wildlife of parenting: the chaotic mornings, the endless negotiations over meals, the scattered toys, the sudden arguments, and the perpetual, exhausting hum of simply keeping tiny humans alive and functioning.
And then, suddenly, they are gone. The house is yours.

In theory, the "night without kids" is the holy grail of modern parenting. It is the mythical oasis you dream about when you are running on three hours of sleep and staring blankly into a lukewarm cup of coffee. It is supposed to be a glorious, uninhibited celebration of your relationship.
But if we are going to be entirely, unapologetically honest about the reality of rebuilding physical intimacy, we have to admit a very difficult truth: an empty house can be utterly terrifying.

When the chaotic noise of the children abruptly stops, it leaves a massive, echoing vacuum in the centre of your home. And in the absence of that noise, the heavy, culturally ingrained script immediately takes over. The script says: The kids are finally gone. This is your one chance. You are supposed to make the most of this. You are supposed to have spectacular, cinematic, hours-long intimacy. If you do not have wild, passionate sex tonight, there is something fundamentally broken about your relationship.

For a nervous system that is just learning how to feel safe again, this expectation is the equivalent of a blazing siren. The empty house, which should be a sanctuary of rest, instantly transforms into a high-pressure performance stage. You look at your partner across the suddenly quiet living room, and instead of feeling a rush of desire, you feel a paralysing grip of performance anxiety. Your jaw locks. Your shoulders hike up to your ears. You suddenly find yourself desperately looking for chores to do—wiping down perfectly clean countertops or folding laundry—just to avoid the agonising pressure of the "opportunity."

If we are going to reclaim our bodies and our voices, we have to completely dismantle the tyranny of the child-free night. We have to burn the script that tells us an empty house is a mandatory invitation for a sexual marathon. We are going to take the empty space, strip it of all its heavy expectations, and turn it into a magnificent playground for connection. We are going to learn how to flirt, how to touch, and how to speak in the quiet, without ever setting a timer on the bomb.

The Masterful Ceasefire: Dropping the Anchor at the Door

The absolute most crucial moment of a night without kids is the very first five minutes. This is the transition zone. If you let the silence hang, the pressure will immediately fill the void. You must take sovereign control of the narrative the second you are alone.

You do this by utilising your voice to drop a statement that simultaneously boosts your partner's ego and explicitly declares a total, unconditional ceasefire on physical demands. Let us look at a masterclass example of this transition. Imagine you have just returned from a rare dinner out. You pull into the driveway, walk up to the front porch, and turn the key. The house is completely dark and wonderfully quiet. As you step inside and drop your keys on the counter, you turn to your partner. You don't use a cheesy, rehearsed pickup line. You don't use heavy, clinical language. You look them directly in the eye, and you deliver the ultimate boundary:
"I had a great time tonight. You looked sexy at dinner. When we get home, I just want to pour a glass of water, lock the door, and exist in the same space as you."
This statement is nothing short of brilliant. Let's break down exactly why this unapologetic approach is so profoundly effective.

First, it delivers the ego boost ("You looked sexy at dinner"). It acknowledges the physical attraction and keeps the energy warm. But then, in the very next breath, it completely annihilates the pressure

("I just want to pour a glass of water... and exist in the same space as you").
By vocalising this out loud, you are proactively defusing the tension. You are looking at the empty, intimidating canvas of the night and declaring it a perfectly safe zone. You are telling your partner that they do not have to perform, they do not have to initiate a grand seduction, and they do not have to worry about letting you down. You are releasing them—and yourself—from the heavy armour of expectation.

When you explicitly remove the goalpost of intercourse, a stunning, miraculous thing happens to the human body. The cortisol drops. The defensive brace in the abdominal muscles releases. The breathing deepens. Because you are no longer terrified of where the night has to end, you are suddenly free to actually enjoy where the night is. The empty house stops being a place of rest and security, becoming a sanctuary where you can finally, truly exhale. A place where you feel comfortable to "Do it."

Unshaming the Domestic Body in the Quiet
One of the most devastating casualties of the gruelling physical reality of parenting is body confidence. When your body has been utilised purely as a functional tool for raising children, it is incredibly easy to disconnect from your own sensuality. We start viewing our bodies as purely utilitarian machines. We notice the exhaustion in our eyes, the shifting weight, and we internalise a quiet, pervasive shame.

When the kids are home, it is easy to hide behind the identity of "Mom" or "Dad." The roles provide a convenient shield. But when the house is empty, those titles are temporarily suspended. You are suddenly just two adults standing in a room. For many, this sudden vulnerability triggers a massive wave of body insecurity.

This is where your voice becomes critical. The empty house is the perfect environment to use your short and sweet banter to aggressively unshame your partner's body, and in doing so, invite them to unshame yours.

We are not talking about reciting polite affirmations in the mirror. We are talking about raw, lighthearted, highly specific appreciation. When you are finally sitting on the couch together, and the only sound is the hum of the refrigerator, do not let the silence breed insecurity. Look over at them. Keep it punchy.
"Your jawline is completely distracting right now."
"Those sweatpants are doing exactly what they need to do."
"You look incredibly good just sitting there."
You are using your words to validate their physical reality in the present moment. You are reminding them that beneath the heavy mantle of their daily responsibilities, they are a deeply attractive, vibrant creature. When you offer this kind of unapologetic praise in a completely safe environment—knowing that you have already declared the ceasefire for the evening—the words penetrate the armour beautifully. They do not feel

like a trick or a prelude to a demand; they feel like genuine, pure validation.

The Housewife to Working Man Dynamic: Playful Role Release

Another phenomenal advantage of the empty house is the ability to temporarily shed the gruelling equality of modern domestic survival and lean into playful, classic dynamics that boost the ego.

When the kids are screaming, the dogs are barking, and the mortgage needs to be paid, the relationship often devolves into a highly stressed logistical partnership. You are co-managers of a chaotic corporation. But when the house is quiet, you can use your voice to step out of the boardroom and into a more playful, deeply appreciative space.

This is where you can lean into the dynamic of provision and care. It is about using short, appreciative statements to validate the sheer effort your partner puts into your shared life, framing their capability not as a boring chore, but as a trait that you find deeply attractive.

While they are sitting on the couch, maybe nursing a beer or a glass of water, you can lean against the back of the sofa, let your hands rest lightly on their shoulders, and say:

"You work so damn hard for us. Just sit there. Let me take care of you tonight."

Or, if they have just finished fixing something around the quiet house:

"Watching you handle things around here does things to me."
You are taking the heavy, often exhausting reality of adulthood and spinning it into gold. You are validating their capability, their strength, and their dedication. By acknowledging their hard work with a flirtatious edge, you are reminding them that you do not just see them as a co-parent or a roommate; you see them as a powerful, capable force in your life, and that capability is a massive turn-on.

The Sensual Micro-Touch: Non-Verbal Talk in the Open Room
As we have established, the most profound communication often bypasses the vocal cords entirely. When the house is completely quiet, the physical senses become hyper-attuned. Without the constant background noise of cartoons, arguments over homework, or the general clatter of family life, the nervous system can suddenly process subtle sensory input with incredible clarity.

This means you do not need grand, sweeping physical gestures to generate warmth. In fact, heavy, aggressive physical contact in a newly quiet house will almost certainly trigger the alarm bells. Instead, we use the Sensual Micro-Touch. A micro-touch is a highly specific, highly intentional, and deeply contained point of physical contact that explores the neutral zones of the body with a brand new, flirtatious energy. It is about waking up the skin without sounding the alarm.

The Palm Trace

The hands are one of the most mechanically complex and neurologically rich areas of the human body. The palm is packed with thousands of sensitive nerve endings, yet it carries absolutely none of the heavy, panic-inducing psychological weight of the chest, the thighs, or the pelvis. Holding hands is generally considered safe, but we are going to elevate it.

While you are sitting next to each other on the couch watching a movie, or just existing in the same space, reach over and take their hand. Turn it palm up. Slowly, deliberately, and with just the right amount of firm pressure, begin to rub your thumb or your index and middle fingers in small, continuous circles directly in the centre of their palm.

Rubbing fingers on the palm of the hand has a profoundly sensual feel. It is deeply grounding, yet simultaneously electric. It commands the attention of the nervous system and draws the focus away from the anxious chatter of the brain and down into the physical reality of the body. You do not need to say a word. The slow, rhythmic friction on their palm is speaking volumes. It is saying, "I am right here. I am touching you. We have all the time in the world."

The Chin Brush

If you want to inject a bit of confident swagger and playful dominance into the quiet room without escalating to full body contact, the chin brush is an unparalleled move.

The skin just under the jawline and the chin is incredibly sensitive. Furthermore, the physical act of lightly guiding someone's head is an inherently intimate, slightly commanding gesture that, when done with extreme gentleness, sends a massive thrill through the body.

If you are standing in the kitchen together, enjoying the silence, or sitting across from each other at the table, reach out with a single hand. Use the soft pad of your index finger to lightly brush right underneath their chin. You can apply just a fraction of an ounce of upward pressure, subtly encouraging them to elevate their gaze and look directly at you.

Keep the contact incredibly brief—just a second or two. Catch their eye, give them a slow smile, deliver a simple "Hi," and let your hand fall away. This micro-touch is electric. It acknowledges their physical presence, it gently commands their attention, and it creates a highly charged moment of connection that requires absolutely zero follow-through.

The Ear Trace
The area around the ear is another magnificent, highly underutilised neutral zone. The skin behind the earlobe and tracing down the very top of the neck is deeply connected to the body's relaxation responses. Light touch here can send shivers down the spine while simultaneously lowering the heart rate.

When you walk past them to grab a blanket, or when you are sitting beside them on the sofa, simply extend a finger and slowly, lightly trace the curve around the back of their ear. You can gently brush their hair out of the way as you do it.

Combine this micro-touch with a verbal compliment for maximum impact. As you trace the curve of their ear, lean in close so they can hear the specific grit in your voice, and whisper, "You look really, really good tonight." Then, pull back, sit down, and resume whatever you were doing. You have just successfully flooded their system with positive sensory emotive, boosted their ego, and reinforced the safety of the empty house all in a single, three-second interaction.

The Power of the Unhurried Night
When you master the art of the ceasefire, the lighthearted banter, and the micro-touch, the empty house completely transforms. It ceases to be a terrifying space where you are expected to perform a high-stakes athletic event, and it becomes a sprawling, luxurious playground where you are free to simply exist.
You realise that true sensuality is not measured by the intensity of the climax, but by the depth of the safety.

A successful night without kids does not have to end in the bedroom. A wildly successful, deeply intimate night can consist entirely of eating takeout food on the coffee table, tracing circles on the palm of your partner's hand, dropping three or four cheeky compliments, and going to sleep feeling completely secure, deeply loved, and entirely unpressured.

By actively removing the goalpost, you give your connection the one thing it desperately needs to grow: time. You prove to yourself, and to your partner, that your bond is resilient, playful, and completely autonomous.

A Gentle Grounding Practice: The Spoken Inventory

This practice is the culmination of everything we have learned about navigating the empty house. It combines the safety of the ceasefire, the ego-boosting power of the spoken word, and the somatic grounding of the micro-touch. It is a highly structured way to practice sensual communication in a completely zero-stakes environment.

Find your sanctuary. Wait until the house is completely quiet and the evening tasks are done. Move to a comfortable, neutral space—the living room couch is usually perfect. You must remain fully clothed. The goal is to maximise comfort and minimise any subconscious anticipation of physical escalation.

The setup. Sit close enough to touch, but do not entangle your bodies. You can sit side-by-side or facing each other with your legs crossed. Take three deep, slow breaths together, letting the residual adrenaline of the day completely drain out of your shoulders.

Declare the boundaries. Before you begin, one of you must explicitly vocalise the ceasefire. Say it out loud into the quiet room: "We are just doing this practice. There are absolutely zero expectations for tonight beyond this moment. I just want to exist in the same space as you."

The physical anchor. The person initiating the practice reaches out and initiates the palm trace. Take your partner's hand, turn it palm up, and begin the slow, deliberate, continuous friction of your fingers against their palm. This physical anchor must remain constant throughout the practice. It provides a steady stream of soothing emotions to the brain, keeping the threat-detection centre offline.

The vocal tour. While maintaining the palm trace, you are going to take turns offering very short, highly specific, unapologetic verbal affirmations of your partner. You are verbally mapping the safe zones of their body and their presence.

The rule is simple: keep it short, keep it sweet, and keep it anchored in the present moment. Do not use therapy-speak. Do not over-explain.

The offering:
Look at your partner and deliver one statement.
"I love the way your shoulders look in that shirt."
"Your jawline is driving me crazy right now."
"You have the most incredible hands."
"Your eyes look really beautiful in this light."

The receipt:

When your partner gives you an offering, your only job is to receive it. You are not allowed to deflect the compliment. You are not allowed to make a self-deprecating joke about your weight or your age. You must simply let the words land.
Take a deep breath, look them in the eye, smile, and say, "Thank you."

Switch roles. Let your partner offer a compliment to you while you maintain the palm trace.
"I am obsessed with the way your hair looks right now."
"You are so incredibly sexy when you are relaxed."
Take a deep breath, absorb the validation, and say, "Thank you."
Continue this back-and-forth for five to ten minutes. You are building a sanctuary of words, block by block, where flirting is safe, fun, and completely free of consequence. You are teaching your body that it is absolutely safe to be adored, and it is absolutely safe to vocalise your desire. You are filling the empty house not with the heavy, anxious demands of performance, but with the warm, resilient, and utterly unapologetic sound of your own voice.

Chapter 5: The Bedroom Sanctuary (Vocalising the Bloom)

For the vast majority of our lives, the bedroom is simply a functional space. It is where we drop our clothes, charge our phones, and surrender to exhaustion at the end of a long day. But when a relationship is actively navigating the complex, often chaotic terrain of intimacy after trauma, the bedroom ceases to be a mere room. It becomes a highly charged, heavy pressure space.

If we are continuing our brutally honest assessment of the healing journey, we must acknowledge the invisible threshold that exists at the bedroom door. You can successfully navigate the Daily Simmer in the kitchen. You can absolutely master the unapologetic swagger of the Passing Graze in the hallway. You can even conquer the Transitional Space of the car, throwing out cheeky micro-flirts with the confidence of a rockstar. But the moment your hand touches the doorknob of the bedroom, a profound psychological shift occurs.

For a nervous system that has been entrenched in survival mode, the bedroom is the room where the "goalpost" lives. It is the room where the heavy, unyielding legislation of performative sex is traditionally enforced. The mattress is not viewed as a place of rest or play; it is viewed as a high-stakes testing ground where you are expected to

deliver a flawless, deeply passionate athletic performance.
Because of this deeply ingrained cultural script, the bedroom has likely been the site of your most profound silences. When you have felt pressured, overwhelmed, or triggered in the past, your body's natural defence mechanism was to shut down the vocal cords. You learned to hold your breath, endure the moment, and stare at the ceiling in complete, suffocating quiet.

Reclaiming your sexual landscape requires a radical, defiant overhaul of this specific geography. You have to take the heavy gavel out of the bedroom, smash the scoreboard to pieces, and declare the space an absolute Sanctuary.
A sanctuary is a place of refuge. It is a place where you are entirely safe from the demands of the outside world. And when you finally step back into this sanctuary with your partner, fully unbound and ready to engage the erotic life force, your most powerful tool for maintaining that safety is you and your playful voice.

This chapter is about Vocalising the Bloom. It is about taking the short, sweet, zero-stakes energy we cultivated in the hallway and bringing it directly between the sheets. It is about dropping the exhausting burden of "dirty talk" and replacing it with real-time, highly effective sensual navigation.

The Myth of the Pornographic Monologue
When we finally feel ready to introduce vocalisation into our physical intimacy, we often immediately sabotage ourselves by referencing

the absolute worst possible source material: cinematic and adult media.

We are culturally conditioned to believe that "sexy talk" in the bedroom requires a highly specific, heavily choreographed script. We think we have to sound like professional actors. We assume we need to deliver breathy, poetic monologues about the depths of our lust, or aggressively explicit demands that feel entirely foreign to our actual personalities.

When you try to wear a vocal costume that doesn't fit you, your nervous system immediately recognises the fraud. The moment you try to force a line that sounds like it belongs in a cheap romance novel, your jaw will lock, your throat will close, and the deeply familiar, panic-inducing wave of awkwardness will wash over you. You will feel ridiculous, and that feeling of ridiculousness will instantly kill the simmer.

Let's be very clear: true, unbridled sensuality does not require a monologue. It does not require a script. In fact, when you are healing, long sentences are the enemy of presence. When you are trying to construct a grammatically correct, highly descriptive sentence about what you are feeling, you are entirely in your head. You have abandoned your body to go play author in your brain.

To vocalise the Bloom, we must return to the absolute brilliance of the lighthearted approach:

keep it short, keep it punchy, and keep it incredibly grounded.

Narrating the Now: The Power of Real-Time Feedback

If you want to completely revolutionise your physical intimacy and massively boost your partner's ego without ever having to memorise a script, you must become a master *of Narrating the Now.*

Narrating the Now is the practice of offering instantaneous, one-to-three-word reviews of the physical emotion you are currently experiencing. It is giving your partner a live, verbal roadmap of what is working.

Think about the psychological reality of your partner in this environment. If they have been weathering the winter alongside you, they are likely walking on eggshells. They are hyper-aware of your past trauma responses. They are terrified of making a wrong move, triggering a freeze response, or pushing a boundary. When the bedroom is completely silent, that silence is agonising for them. They have absolutely no idea if what they are doing feels good or if you are simply holding your breath and enduring it. When you break that silence with a short, affirmative statement, it is like throwing a lifeline to a drowning sailor. It offers them immediate, undeniable proof that they are on the right track, which allows them to finally relax and enjoy the moment themselves.

You do not need to be poetic. You just need to be honest, and you need to drop it with a little bit of swagger.

When their hand moves to a spot that feels genuinely good, you do not need to explain the somatic release occurring in your body. You just lean your head back and say:

"Right there."

When the rhythm of their touch perfectly matches the slow, steady simmer of your nervous system, you lock eyes with them for a second and say:

"Don't stop."

When you feel that deep, primal spark of electricity flare up in your chest because of the way they are looking at you, you offer the simplest, most devastatingly sexy phrase in the English language:

"Mmm. Yes."

These tiny, microscopic vocalisations are the ultimate game-changers. They require virtually zero mental energy to produce, but they yield a massive return on investment. They validate your partner's efforts, they keep your own brain tethered directly to the physical sensation of the present moment, and they flood the room with a highly charged, undeniable energy. You are not performing; you are simply reporting live from a deeply pleasurable sanctuary.

The Playful Command: Reclaiming the Active Voice

Trauma is inherently an experience of powerlessness. It is an event, or a series of events, where your sovereignty was violently or systematically stripped away from you. Because of this, many survivors unconsciously adopt a deeply passive role in their intimate lives. We become the passenger. We lay back, hold our breath, and wait to see what our partner will do, constantly bracing for impact.

Reclaiming your sexual landscape means taking your hands firmly off your chest and putting them directly on the steering wheel. It means transitioning from a passive receiver to an active, sovereign architect of your own pleasure. And the most effective way to do this is through the Playful Command.

A Playful Command is a short, confident, zero-stakes instruction. It is the rock-and-roll swagger of knowing exactly what you want and unapologetically asking for it, without any heavy, serious demands.
Again, this is a massive relief for your partner. When you give them a direct instruction, you completely remove the terrifying burden of guesswork. You are not giving them an ultimatum; you are handing them an engraved invitation to succeed.

The Playful Command is delivered with a smirk, a completely relaxed posture, and total confidence. If you are lying on the bed and you want to feel the weight of them against you, do not silently wait and hope they figure it out. Tap the mattress beside you, look them in the eye, and say: "Come here."

If they are touching your arm and you want them to move to your neck, do not sit in passive frustration. Gently take their hand, move it to the exact spot you want, and whisper:
"Touch me", "Right here."
If the room feels a little too serious and you want to inject some unapologetic heat into the atmosphere, look at the t-shirt they are wearing, give them a slow, appreciative once-over, and drop a confident:
"Take that shirt off for me."

These commands are not about BDSM, dominance, or heavy power dynamics. In the context of the Daily Simmer and the Bedroom Sanctuary, the Playful Command is simply about un-shaming your own desire. It is the vocalisation of your absolute right to take up space, to have preferences, and to direct the flow of traffic in your own ecosystem. Fun and incredibly empowering.

Unshaming the Soundtrack: Breath, Laughter, and the Hum
We must also radically expand our definition of what constitutes a "voice" in the bedroom. Words are only a fraction of our communicative arsenal. The rest of the soundtrack is composed of the raw, unfiltered acoustic emotions of the human body: the breath, the sigh, the moan, and the laugh.

During the protective winter, the body's natural response to anxiety is to restrict oxygen. We engage the abdominal brace, we lock our diaphragms, and we breathe shallowly into the very top of our chests. We become entirely silent. This silence is a brilliant survival tactic when hiding from a predator in the wild, but it is absolute poison to physical intimacy.

To vocalise the Bloom, you must consciously, deliberately unbind your breath, and you must give yourself radical permission to make noise.
You do not have to perform the exaggerated, theatrical sounds of adult media. You simply have to stop suppressing the genuine physical reactions of your own body.

When your partner touches you in a way that feels grounding and safe, do not swallow the sigh of relief. Let it out. Let it be a long, audible, open-mouthed exhale.

When you experience a flash of genuine pleasure, lean into the Vocal Hum we practised earlier. Let that low, resonant "hmmmm" vibrate in the back of your throat. That sound is not a word, but it is one of the most powerful, ego-boosting micro-flirts in existence. It bypasses the intellectual brain entirely and speaks directly to your partner's primal nervous system, signalling absolute success and safety.

The Comedy of Errors: The Power of the Mid-Act Laugh
There is a bizarre, deeply unhelpful expectation that physical intimacy must be a flawless, perfectly choreographed ballet. But when you are dealing with two highly complex human bodies, tangled

limbs, shifting weights, and the sheer mechanics of gravity, things are going to go wrong. Foreheads will inevitably bump. Knees will collide. Someone will accidentally lean on the TV remote and blast a random infomercial at maximum volume. The dog will suddenly decide that right now is the perfect time to burst into the room and aggressively lick someone's foot.

For a traumatised ecosystem, these sudden, unexpected disruptions can be catastrophic. The sudden jarring movement or the break in concentration can instantly activate the threat-detection centre. The brain registers the disruption, assumes the environment is no longer safe, and slams the emergency brakes. The moment is ruined, and the heavy, silent shame descends.

This is where your voice becomes your ultimate shield and your greatest unbinder.
When the clumsy reality of human existence interrupts your sanctuary, you must brutally reject the urge to freeze. You must actively, loudly, and unapologetically introduce humour into the room.

Humour is the ultimate physiological reset button. It is physically impossible to be in a state of primal fear while you are genuinely laughing. Laughter floods the brain with a massive rush of endorphins, completely neutralising the cortisol spike of the unexpected disruption.

If you attempt a smooth, sexy manoeuvre and end up awkwardly tumbling off the edge of the

mattress, do not apologise profusely. Do not retreat into your shell. Roll over onto your back, look up at the ceiling, and laugh out loud. Look at your partner and drop that zero-stakes comment: "Well, that was spectacularly uncoordinated."
If teeth accidentally clack together during a kiss, pull back, smirk, and say:
"Clearly, I missed the lesson on basic physics today." – a line enough to make anyone laugh or maybe choke.

By vocalising the humour of the situation, you are actively managing the energy of the room. You are telling your partner—and your own skittish nervous system—that this is not a high-stakes performance review. It is just two people, completely safe, having a ridiculous, messy, beautiful time together. You are cementing the fact that the bedroom is a playground, not a stage.

The Daylight Swagger: The Kid-Free Morning Rebellion

There is a glorious extension to the child-free night, and that is the child-free morning. The sun comes up, the house is still miraculously quiet, and the heavy mantle of parental responsibility hasn't quite settled back onto your shoulders yet. This is prime real estate for the ultimate daylight swagger.
When the kids are home, mornings are a frantic scramble to find shoes, make lunches, pack backpacks, and shout over the noise. You dress quickly, hiding behind bathroom doors. But in the empty clearing? The rules are completely suspended.

If you want to completely unshame your body and keep the pot simmering right into breakfast, you have to embrace the Morning Rebellion. It is about taking the Bedroom Sanctuary's playful, uninhibited energy and dragging it directly into the bright morning light.

Imagine your partner is sitting at the kitchen island, staring blearily at their phone while the coffee brews. Instead of shuffling in wearing your oldest, most oversized bathrobe, you stride into the kitchen completely naked on your way to the shower.

You don't make a big, serious production out of it. You just walk in, pour yourself a cup of coffee, give them a cheeky smirk, and confidently walk out. It completely shatters the mundane tension and reminds your partner that you are not just a co-parent; you are a vibrant, bold, deeply fun creature who is entirely comfortable in your/their own skin.
Or, if you are getting dressed for the day and they are still lying in bed scrolling through the news, you can use the ultimate physical micro-flirt. You pull off your pyjamas, turn around, and casually flick your g-string right at their chest.
You drop a quick, cheeky, "Morning, Sexy," as it lands, and walk into the bathroom.
It is hilarious. It is shocking in the absolute best way. It proves that the erotic life force doesn't evaporate the second the sun comes up, and it completely rewrites the heavy, exhausted script of domestic mornings.

The Afterglow: The Final Micro-Flirt
The way you use your voice immediately after a
period of physical connection—whether that
connection resulted in intercourse, a prolonged
session of the palm trace, or just an hour of deeply
connected, clothed parallel play—is critical for
setting the baseline temperature for the rest of the
day.
The immediate aftermath of intimacy is often a
vulnerable space. The body is flooded with
oxytocin, the "bonding hormone," which makes us
feel deeply connected but also highly susceptible
to sudden shifts in tone.

The old script might demand a deep, emotional,
hour-long conversation about your feelings. But
remember, we are operating in the realm of the
Daily Simmer. We want to keep it light, confident,
and profoundly secure. We do not need to
overprocess the moment.

As you settle back into the pillows, or as you sit up
to take a sip of water, offer one final, definitive
micro-flirt. This is the closing parenthesis on the
interaction. It is the stamp of approval that allows
the nervous system to fully power down and
transition into rest.
Keep it simple. Keep it, Joey.
"That was exactly what I needed."
Or simply, placing a hand on their chest, looking at
them with a relaxed smile, and whispering:
"You are incredible."
Deliver the line, close your eyes, and go to sleep.
You do not need to wait for a profound response.

You have spoken your truth, you have validated their existence, and you have successfully maintained the beautiful, sustainable heat of the simmer.

The Sovereign Voice
When you finally realise that your voice is not a fragile, dangerous thing that must be hidden away, the entire architecture of your relationship changes. You are no longer a passive participant in your own life. You are a sovereign, fully unbound creator.

You learn that you can be incredibly sexy without ever memorising a script. You learn that a single, unapologetic "You cute" thrown across the kitchen island holds infinitely more power than a forced, uncomfortable monologue in the dark. You discover that your actual, authentic voice—with all its clunkiness, its laughter, and its beautiful imperfections—is exactly what your partner has been desperate to hear.

The winter is over. The ice has thawed. The roots are secure in the soil.
It is time to step fully into the wide, unbothered sky of your own sensuality. It is time to open the door to the sanctuary, drop the heavy armour on the floor, and let the canopy of your forest finally, beautifully, and loudly whisper in the wind.

A Gentle Grounding Practice: The Sensory Echo
This final somatic practice is designed to help you explicitly connect your physical sensation to your

vocal cords, bridging the gap between feeling an experience and confidently speaking it out loud in the Bedroom Sanctuary.

The setup. Lay comfortably on your bed with your partner. You can be fully clothed or not, depending entirely on the current comfort level of your ecosystem. The only requirement is that you are physically touching in a safe, non-demanding way—perhaps your legs are tangled, or you are resting your head on their chest.

The anchor. Close your eyes. Take three deep, slow belly breaths, actively releasing any residual tension in your jaw and your shoulders. Allow the mattress to fully support your weight.

The sensory scan. Keeping your eyes closed, bring your entire conscious attention to the specific point where your body is touching your partner's body. Let's say their hand is resting gently on your stomach.

Gather the emotive. Focus entirely on the raw physical emotion of that specific point of contact. What is the temperature of their hand? Is it warm? What is the weight of it? What is the texture of their skin against yours? Do not judge the feeling; simply observe it as an absolute, irrefutable fact.

The internal echo. Once you have locked onto the physical sensation, translate that feeling into a single, three-word sentence inside your head. Make it a factual report of your current reality.

Silently think: "Your hand is warm." Or, "This feels very safe."

The vocalisation. Take a deep breath in. As you slowly exhale, gently push that internal thought out through your vocal cords. Do not open your eyes. Do not change your tone to sound "sexy." Just speak the truth of the sensation into the quiet room.

Whisper: "Your hand feels really good right there."

The receipt. Your partner does not need to respond with a compliment or escalate the touch. Their only job is to receive the emotive. They can simply take a deep breath in tandem with you, or offer a very quiet, "I'm glad."

The repetition. Shift your focus to a different sensory input. Listen to the sound of their breathing. Feel the vibration of their chest. Create the internal sentence. "Your heartbeat is steady." Speak it out loud.

By practising the Sensory Echo, you are training your brain to bypass the panic-inducing filter of performance anxiety. You are proving that you do not need to invent a script; the script is already written by the physical reality of your own body. You are simply learning how to read it out loud.

Conclusion: The Loud, Beautiful, and Unapologetic Spring

There is a profound, almost reckless bravery in choosing to make a sound after you have spent a lifetime perfecting the art of silence.

When you have weathered a brutal, deeply protective winter—when your nervous system has learned that the safest way to survive intimacy is to hold your breath, lock your jaw, and endure—learning how to speak again is not just a milestone. It is an absolute rebellion. It is a declaration of your own sovereignty.

Take a moment to look back at the landscape you have traversed. In our first journey together, you did the quiet, agonising work of unbinding the body. You sat with the weight of your empty hands. You dismantled the heavy iron armour of societal expectations and removed the terrifying, panic-inducing goalpost of the traditional sexual staircase. You gave yourself radical, unconditional permission to simply exist in the quiet clearing of your own forest.

But as the ice thawed and the sap of the new spring began to rise, we encountered the final, most stubborn ghost of the winter: the frozen voice. We realised that feeling the spark of the erotic life force is only half the battle; knowing how to translate that spark into unapologetic, zero-stakes communication can truly bring the mojo back to life.

Throughout this second book, we have systematically burned the old, exhausting scripts to the ground. We took the cinematic, heavily choreographed "dirty talk" monologue—the one that requires you to play a hyper-confident, flawless actor—and threw it out the window. We replaced it with the raw, gritty, incredibly fun reality of your actual, unvarnished personality.

We learned that you do not need to speak in poetic paragraphs to generate heat. You just need the swagger of a micro-flirt. You need the simple, devastating effectiveness of catching your partner's eye across the kitchen and dropping a classic "How you doin'?" You need the confidence to walk past them in the hallway, give their hip a gentle squeeze, and deliver a completely zero-stakes "Sexy ass" before walking away.

We dragged intimacy out of the dark, high-pressure confines of the midnight bedroom and let it run wild in the bright, messy reality of the daily routine. We turned the kitchen sink into a playground for the Daily Simmer. We transformed the contained, forward-moving pod of the car into a mobile sanctuary for building anticipation. We took back the terrifying void of the "kid-free night," stripping away the heavy demands and replacing them with the masterful ceasefire, the sensual palm trace, and the absolute hilarity of flicking a g-string across the bedroom.

You have built a completely new vocabulary. But as we close this chapter of the journey, there are a

few final, vital truths you must anchor into your
soil.

The Myth of the Finish Line
When we embark on a journey of healing, our
deeply conditioned, goal-oriented brains
immediately start searching for the finish line. We
want to know exactly when we will be "cured." We
want a certificate that says we have successfully
graduated from trauma recovery, guaranteeing
that we will never experience a locked jaw, a
sudden wave of panic, or an awkward moment of
silence ever again.

*I need you to listen to me very carefully: The
finish line is a lie.*

Healing a traumatised ecosystem is not a linear
march toward a permanent, flawless state of
blissful perfection. If you expect to reach a point
where every single micro-flirt lands perfectly,
where your voice never cracks, and where you are
operating at maximum sensual swagger 365 days
a year, you are setting yourself up for a massive,
devastating failure.

Relationships are living, breathing, wildly
unpredictable organisms. Bodies get exhausted.
The stress of the outside world creeps in. The
mortgage is due, the car breaks down, and the
kids get the flu. There will be days when the Daily
Simmer feels entirely out of reach, and the
absolute best you can manage is a tired nod
across the living room.

There will also be moments when the ghost of the winter briefly returns. You might be in the middle of a beautiful, deeply connected moment in the Bedroom Sanctuary, and completely out of nowhere, a sudden shadow will cross your nervous system. Your throat will tighten. The "Third Entity" of past trauma will try to slam the gate shut.
This is not a failure. This is not a relapse. This is simply the weather.

When the sudden frost hits, you no longer have to panic. You do not have to retreat into the heavy armour of shame, and you do not have to fake your way through the rest of the evening. Because you now own your voice, you have the ultimate weapon against the frost. You simply open your mouth and use it.

You look at your partner, you take a deep breath, and you say: "I just got a little overwhelmed. I need a minute. Just hold my hand."
Do you understand the immense power of that statement? By vocalising the frost, you immediately strip it of its power. You prove to your threat-detection centre that you are no longer a hostage to the panic. You are the architect of the moment. You can hit the pause button whenever you damn well please. And when you realise that you have the absolute right to say "stop" without destroying the relationship, your "yes" and your "mmmhhhmmm" become infinitely more powerful, authentic, and free.

The Ego Boost as a Currency of Connection

If there is one profound, lasting habit you take away from The Whispering Canopy, let it be the relentless, generous application of the ego boost. For so long, the focus of your healing journey has understandably been internal. You had to focus entirely on your own nervous system, your own boundaries, and your own survival. But as the spring returns, the focus beautifully expands outward.

Your partner has been standing in the clearing with you. They have held space for the silence. They have navigated the confusing, often painful withdrawal of physical connection. As you step fully into your vocal sovereignty, use your voice to aggressively, playfully unshame them.

Make it a daily practice to remind them of their inherent, undeniable magnetism. Do not hoard your compliments. If you think they look good in a pair of jeans, do not just think it—say it. If the way they handle a stressful phone call turns you on, tell them. If you love the sound of their gravelly voice in the morning, make sure they know it. When you consistently feed the mojo with these short, punchy, zero-stakes validations, you create an impenetrable fortress of mutual appreciation. You build a relationship that is so completely saturated in playful warmth that the cold winds of the outside world simply cannot penetrate it. You become a team of rockstars, deeply invested in hyping each other up.

The Comedy of Survival
Never, ever lose the laughter.

If we have learned anything from the clumsy, beautiful reality of unshaming the voice, it is that humour is the ultimate unbinder. The pursuit of perfect, cinematic intimacy is a toxic trap. Real intimacy is messy. It is uncoordinated. It is knocking over a glass of water on the nightstand, accidentally head-butting each other in the dark, and walking into the kitchen completely naked just to see the shocked, delighted look on their face. When you can look at the chaotic, unpredictable reality of human bodies colliding and choose to laugh out loud, you have achieved the highest echelon of trauma recovery. Laughter is the sound of a nervous system that knows, with absolute certainty, that it is safe.

Let your sensual voice be laced with a smirk. Let your micro-flirts be a little bit ridiculous. Allow yourself to be the Joey Tribbiani of your own household—unapologetically confident, relentlessly playful, and entirely unbothered by the pressure to be perfect.

The Canopy Awaits
You have spent enough time in the silence. You have paid your dues to the winter, and you have done the gruelling work of tending to the soil. The heavy, iron legislation of how you are "supposed" to talk, how you are "supposed" to touch, and how you are "supposed" to desire has been completely repealed. You are the sole, sovereign author of your own physical reality. Look around your ecosystem. The trees are tall, the roots are deep, and the clearing is bathed in the warm, golden light of the Daily Simmer. It is

your space. It belongs entirely to you and the
partner you have chosen to share it with.
Do not be afraid of the sound of your own desire.
Do not shrink back from the electric, dirty, sexy
reality of your own swagger. The world has told
you for far too long that your body is a problem to
be solved, and that your voice is something that
should be polite, quiet, and heavily managed.
Reject that completely. Step into the centre of the
clearing. Take a deep, massive breath of air all the
way down into your belly. Feel the vibration of
your own life force humming in your throat.
And then, let it out. Let it be a whisper, let it be a
laugh, let it be a cheeky, passing compliment in
the hallway. Just let the canopy hear you.
The spring is here, and it is beautifully,
unapologetically loud.

Appendix: Quick Reference

A Practical Guide to Sexual Communication and Gentle Exploration:

• Drop a classic "How you doin'?" or "You cute" when walking past them (Ch 1).

• Give a passing graze in a narrow hallway with a cheeky smile (Ch 2).

• Send a mid-day text: "You looked incredibly good leaving the house today" (Ch 2).

• Play the Silent Observer: lean against the doorframe and just watch them shower (Ch 2).

• Admire their driving: "The way your hands grip that steering wheel..." (Ch 3).

• Rest your open hand palm-up on the car's centre console (Ch 3).

• Declare the Masterful Ceasefire when the house is empty: "Zero expectations tonight" (Ch 4).

• Try the Palm Trace: slowly rub circles in the centre of their hand while sitting together (Ch 4).

• Use the Chin Brush or Ear Trace to send a shiver down their spine (Ch 4).

• Narrate the Now in the bedroom: Keep it to "Right there" or "Mmm. Yes" (Ch 5).

• Embrace the Comedy of Errors: Laugh out loud when foreheads bump, or things get clumsy! (Ch 5).

• Execute the Daylight Swagger: Walk into the kitchen naked for coffee, or flick a g-string at them (Ch 5).

Want to initiate and escalate the heat?

Bring your own tone to these short and sweet demands.

- "Wanna, do it."

- "Take down your pants" (action = physical or verbal)

- "Let's *bang*" (*screw, make love, ride, slide, play, f***, etc*)

- "Hi" (action = wink, slide hand over body)

- "One taste of you"

- "You and Me after dinner?" (action = wink, slide hand over body)

- "Desert" (action = wink, slide hand over body)

- "Sexy Time"

- "Hey" (action = wink, slide hand over body)

- "Touch it" (song, action = physical or verbal)

- "Taste me – Taste you?"

- "What you doin?" (action = drop a clothing item)

- "Patient, Nurse?" (scenario play)

- "6 – 9"

- "*Take* me" (*Suck, Fuck, etc*)

Beginner's Guide to Sex Therapy Series

116

Series Overview: Talk 2 Me – Beginner's Guide to Sex Therapy Series

By Marcia Anita Hobbs

Welcome to the Talk 2 Me - Beginner's Guide to Sex Therapy Series, a comprehensive, multi-volume collection designed to completely dismantle the heavy, manufactured expectations surrounding human intimacy and physical connection. Authored by Marcia Anita Hobbs—a newly qualified sex therapy practitioner whose multidisciplinary background spans from aquatics and somatic movement to fierce human rights advocacy—this series serves as a highly accessible extension of her exclusive online counselling practice.

Spanning numerous books, this collection serves as a foundational library addressing a vast array of topics across the entire spectrum of sex therapy. From exploring the biological reality of the nervous system's protective responses and navigating the gentle nuances of somatic touch, to redefining communication within a shared relationship and actively unshaming the body, each instalment provides a vital, standalone piece of the puzzle.

Bringing a distinctly gritty, witty, and deeply compassionate voice to the complex landscape of sexual health and recovery, this collection rejects the clinical coldness often found in traditional self-help resources. Instead, it offers a sovereign-based, trauma-informed approach that honours the human body as a dynamic, deeply intelligent ecosystem rather than a broken machine.

What to Expect from the Series

A Broad Scope of Exploration: A continuously expanding collection covering diverse, highly relevant aspects of modern sex therapy, sensual exploration, and psychological unbinding.
Accessible Digital Integration: Crafted specifically to complement online, self-directed healing, allowing readers to engage with profound therapeutic concepts from the absolute safety and privacy of their own personal spaces.
Somatic and Sovereign Focus: Practical, grounding frameworks designed to help readers reconnect with their physical forms, establish uncompromising personal boundaries, and communicate their needs without guilt.

The Beginner's Guide to Sex Therapy Series is your trusted, step-by-step field guide. It is an open invitation to stop forcing a performance, lay down the gavel of self-judgment, and gently reclaim your sexual landscape on your own timeline.

'Fear Is The Root Of All Weakness®'

An individual is not subject to any civil, criminal or administrative liability for making a public interest disclosure.
It is an offence to take a reprisal, or to threaten to take a reprisal, against a person because of a public interest disclosure (including a proposed or a suspected public interest disclosure).
The Federal Court or Federal Circuit Court may make orders for civil remedies (including compensation, injunctions and reinstatement of employment) if a reprisal is taken against a person because of a public interest disclosure (including a proposed or a suspected public interest disclosure).
It is an offence to disclose the identity of an individual who makes a public interest disclosure.

Public Interest Disclosure Act 2013
No. 133, 2013
(Part 2; Subdivision A—Immunity from liability)

www.ingramcontent.com/pod-product-compliance
Lightning Source LLC
Chambersburg PA
CBHW050033040726

47599CB00015B/1653